Religions of the World

Hinduism

Titles in the Religions of the World series include:

Buddhism

Confucianism

Hinduism

Islam

Shinto

Hinduism

Thomas Streissguth

Lucent Books, Inc.
10911 Technology Place, San Diego, California, 92127

Library of Congress Cataloging-in-Publication Data

Streissguth, Thomas, 1958–
    Hinduism / by Thomas Streissguth.
        p. cm. — (Religions of the world)
Includes bibliographical references and index.
    ISBN 1-56006-985-6 (hardback : alk. paper)
1. Hinduism—Juvenile literature. I. Title. II. Religions of the world
(San Diego, Calif.)
BL1203 .S77 2002
294.5—dc21

2001005697

Contents

Foreword

Religion has always been a central component of human culture, though its form and practice have changed through time. Ancient people lived in a world they could not explain or comprehend. Their world consisted of an environment controlled by vague and mysterious powers attributed to a wide array of gods. Artifacts dating to a time before recorded history suggest that the religion of the distant past reflected this world, consisting mainly of rituals devised to influence events under the control of these gods.

The steady advancement of human societies brought about changes in religion as in all other things. Through time, religion came to be seen as a system of beliefs and practices that gave meaning to—or allowed acceptance of—anything that transcended the natural or the known. And, the belief in many gods ultimately was replaced in many cultures by the belief in a Supreme Being.

As in the distant past, however, religion still provides answers to timeless questions: How, why, and by whom was the universe created? What is the ultimate meaning of human life? Why is life inevitably followed by death? Does the human soul continue to exist after death, and if so, in what form? Why is there pain and suffering in the world, and why is there evil?

In addition, all the major world religions provide their followers with a concrete and clearly stated ethical code. They offer a set of moral instructions, defining virtue and evil and what is required to achieve goodness. One of these universal moral codes is compassion toward others above all else. Thus, Judaism, Christianity, Islam, Hinduism, Buddhism, Confucianism, and Taoism each teach a version of the so-called golden rule, or in the words of Jesus Christ, "As ye would that men should do to you, do ye also to them likewise." (Luke 6:31) For example, Confucius instructed his disciples to "never impose on others what you would not choose for yourself." (*Analects:* 12:2) The Hindu epic poem, Mahabharata, identifies the core of all Hindu teaching as not doing unto others what you do not wish done to yourself. Similarly Muhammad declared that no Muslim could be a true believer unless he desired for his brother no less than that which he desires for himself.

It is ironic, then, that although compassionate concern for others forms the heart of all the major religions' moral teachings, religion has also been at the root of countless conflicts throughout history. It has been suggested that much of the appeal that religions hold for humankind lies in their unswerving faith in the truth of their particular vision. Throughout history, most religions have shared a profound confidence that their interpretation of life, God, and the universe is the right one, thus giving their followers a sense of certainty in an uncertain and often fragile existence. Given the assurance displayed by most religions regarding the fundamental correctness of their teachings and practices, it is perhaps not surprising that religious intolerance has fueled disputes and even full-scale wars between peoples and nations time and time again, from the Crusades of medieval times to the current bloodshed in Northern Ireland and the Middle East.

Today, as violent religious conflicts trouble many parts of our world, it has become more important than ever to learn about the similarities as well as the differences between faiths. One of the most effective ways to accomplish this is by examining the beliefs, customs, and values of various religions. In the Religions of the World series, students will find a clear description of the core creeds, rituals, ethical teachings, and sacred texts of the world's major religions. In-depth explorations of how these faiths changed over time, how they have influenced the social customs, laws, and education of the countries in which they are practiced, and the particular challenges each one faces in coming years are also featured.

Extensive quotations from primary source materials, especially the core scriptures of each faith, and a generous number of secondary source quotations from the works of respected modern scholars are included in each volume in the series. It is hoped that by gaining insight into the faiths of other peoples and nations, students will not only gain a deeper appreciation and respect for different religious beliefs and practices, but will also gain new perspectives on and understanding of their own religious traditions.

The Elusive Faith

When non-Hindus try to understand the world religion of Hinduism, they often have trouble applying the word *Hinduism* to a single set of beliefs, a single god, or a single system of worship or set of rituals. For many, Hinduism conjures stories of mythical heroes and the images of gods, each associated with characteristic dress, attributes, expression, and colors. Temples, shrines, and holy places—built in hundreds of different styles—reflect the public practice of Hinduism, while a visit to a Hindu household may reveal its private devotion in a quiet niche decorated with pictures of a god, surrounded by flowers, food offerings, and incense sticks.

For instruction in the religion, readers may turn to ancient Hindu texts such as the *Mahabharata,* the *Ramayana,* and the Bhagavad Gita. Yet these works form just a small part of the literature of Hindu belief. Various Hindu sects teach particular ways of life and thought, and the lessons of Hindu philosophers have been set down in an enormous array of books.

At first glance, Hinduism may appear inextricably tied to the subcontinent of India, and certainly mention of this faith evokes powerful scenes set there: Sacred cows stroll the streets of villages, while in the distance funeral pyres burn beside a river strewn with flowers and crowded with people bathing in its waters. But in fact, Hinduism has spread to every continent.

There are large communities of Hindu believers in England; Hindus have also settled in eastern Africa and throughout southern Asia, where merchants brought their beliefs as well as their trading goods centuries ago; and although Islam dominates most of what is now Indonesia, Hinduism remains strong on the island of Bali, where believers created a unique mythology and ritual practice.

A clear-cut definition of Hinduism eludes students and historians. Some writers even deny that there is a single Hindu religion. Instead, they believe that the term *Hinduism* defines a culture rather than a religious faith. Bruce M. Sullivan, in his *Historical Dictionary of Hinduism*, declares:

Whether Hinduism is one religion or several is to some extent dependent on how one defines the term "religion." If a religion must, of necessity, have a single theology, the same object of worship for all devotees, and an agreed-upon

A Hindu merchant finds a quiet place to pray.

canon of scripture, it would seem that Hinduism is not one religion, but several.[1]

Others see in Hinduism not a faith but a valuable mental exercise, a way of training and focusing the mind that evolved out of an ancient religion. For example, the philosophies of yoga, described by many Hindu teachers, have been adopted by non-Indians who have no knowledge of the Hindu gods. Joseph Campbell, a noted student and teacher of mythology, defines yoga this way:

The ancient postures of yoga have been carved into this temple wall in Indonesia.

I imagine that when one thinks of Indian philosophy the first thought is of yoga. . . . Take into your mind an image . . . and try to hold this image still in your mind. You will find that you are immediately thinking of other images, associated with the first; for the mind continues spontaneously to move. Yoga is the intentional stopping of this spontaneous activity of the mind. . . . The notion is that what we see when we look around, like this, are the broken images of a perfect form. And what is that form? It is the form of a divine reality, which appears to us only in broken images when our mind stuff is in action.[2]

In other words, yoga is not a faith in itself, but a means to an end: the viewing of something beyond ordinary reality and everyday life.

Coining a Word

Although the beliefs of Hinduism date back thousands of years, *Hinduism* as a word denoting these beliefs is very recent, originating in the early nineteenth century. And the term did not come from believers; instead, it was created by the British, who occupied and governed India at that time, and who needed a convenient word to signify the religious faith and practices of their subjects. The British, however, applied the name broadly, and eventually *Hindu* came to mean anyone who lived in India but who was not Muslim. It was also applied outside the colony to people who adhered to the gods and practices of believers in India.

For their part, India's Hindus consider theirs to be a highly inclusive faith, one that encompasses a vast array of beliefs. Indira Gandhi, who served as prime minister of independent India during the 1960s, 1970s, and 1980s, points out in her book *Eternal India* that Hinduism offers something for every individual, no matter what his or her temperament:

> There is the spiritual man, for whom Indian religion provides an utter freedom from all dogma, ceremony and creed. . . . There is the intellectual man, to whom are offered different systems of knowledge, countless philosophies and unending literature of commentaries and commentaries on commentaries. There is the vital man, the man of emotion, passion and action, for whom there is a vast literature of stories. . . . Finally, there is the physical man for whom Indian religion is a system of outer symbols and rituals, of festivals and other such occasions which, even in his daily routine, bring him into contact with the deeper truths that govern the cosmos.[3]

Hinduism may be very difficult to define and completely understand, but in a world suffering from long-lasting—and now very dangerous—conflicts among nations, cultures, and religions, it does at least hold out the promise of mutual respect and tolerance.

chapter | one

The Origins of the Hindu Faith

Hinduism has a presence and influence around the world. It also has one of the longest histories of any world religion; the foundations of Hindu belief go back nearly five millennia. In their prayers and hymns, modern Hindus are reciting the literature of ancient priests who formed a caste of conquering nobles in the Indus River Valley. Their oldest sacred literature, the Rig-Veda, dates from around 1500 B.C., making it the oldest holy book still in common use anywhere in the world. During wedding ceremonies, seasonal festivals, and solemn funerals, Hindus may hear the hymns of the Rig-Veda and take steps around a sacred fire, a ritual that can be traced to the Indo-Europeans, or "Aryans," a group that wrought a transformation in the Indus Valley more than three thousand years ago.

Some historians assert that Hinduism, or the "Vedic" religion with which it began, closely resembles the beliefs held by the Indo-European peoples who later populated Europe, the Middle East, and western Asia. According to this view, ancient Hinduism may have been the faith from which Judaism, Christianity, and other faiths later evolved among far-flung peoples in very different ages and circumstances.

The modern discovery of ancient Indian civilization began in a hot, dusty river valley in 1856. While digging and blasting near the Indus River, John and William Brunton, two English railroad engineers, came across the ruins of an old brick city, named Harappa. Archaeologists who came to the site in the Indus Valley, located in what is now Pakistan, realized that a very wealthy and highly developed civilization once flourished there. The streets of the city were laid out in ruler-straight lines, designed to intersect at right angles; the largest houses had several dozen rooms and a series of inner courtyards. The ruins were unlike anything ever seen on the Indian subcontinent, and historians realized that an entirely new chapter of the world's history would have to be written.

At the height of what is known as the Indus Valley culture, Harappa and another city known as Mohenjo-Daro each covered an area of about one square mile, and contained as many as fifty thousand people. The citadel of Mohenjo-Daro was circled by a wall fifty feet high, with high defensive towers and gates. At Harappa a large granary, two hundred feet long, was

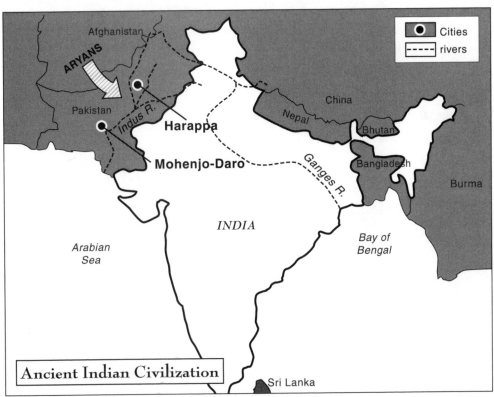

Ancient Indian Civilization

used to store rich harvests of wheat and barley.

Despite its richness, little remains to tell of the Indus Valley culture. Over several millennia, the heavy rains and floods that periodically visit the region have destroyed nearly all traces of the homes and marketplaces that crowded the fertile valley. No books, few works of art, and only scattered household artifacts, such as pottery, tools, sculpture, and jewelry, survive to testify about the people and their way of life. Most importantly, the alphabet used here has defeated every attempt by archaeologists and linguists to decipher it. The records that remain, in the form of clay seals, do not reveal what the people of the Indus Valley experienced or how they lived. As historian Sinharaja Tammita-Delgoda explains:

The Indus script has a total of 400 characters and consists mainly of pictures, which denote a symbol or idea of some kind. Its appearance is very stiff and precise, rather like the hieroglyphic script of Egypt. It consists of a series of brief inscriptions, never more than twenty symbols and usually no more than ten. . . . Over the years many attempts have been made by many different scholars to decipher these Indus symbols. All such efforts have failed completely and the script still remains a total mystery.[4]

The Indus Valley civilization poses many more tough puzzles for historians and archaeologists. Following the discovery of the city, the old bricks of Harappa crumbled into dust, and the

Ruins are all that remain of the brick city of Harappa (left). A seal depicting a bull standing by an incense burner is one of many artifacts found here.

engineers who discovered Harappa reused much of what they found for building their railroad. But this all took place long after another enemy, a group of chariot-driving nomads from the dusty plains far to the north, accomplished the worst destruction around 1500 B.C.

The Aryan Conquest

A majority of historians agree that a people known as Aryans originated in the sweeping plains that lie north of the Black Sea and the Caspian Sea, in what is modern-day Russia and Ukraine. At some point, about four thousand years ago, this people divided into two groups and began a gradual migration. One group went west, to settle in what is now Europe; another group went south and then east. Eventually, the eastbound Aryans reached the flat, fertile Indus Valley, an immense region that covers what is today northwestern India and Pakistan.

According to most historians, the already-declining Indus Valley civilization could not resist the more powerful armies of the Aryans. These newcomers gradually absorbed the Indus Valley peoples, established Sanskrit as the primary language, and made an inferior social class of the conquered peoples. The Aryans built chariots—which gave them a strong advantage in battle—and bred horses for work and for warfare.

They organized themselves into tribes, one of the most powerful of which was known as the Bharatas. This name would take on great importance in Hindu literature.

Historians who accept this account of how a foreign people invaded the Indus Valley, bringing with them their own religion and culture, point to certain passages in the Rig-Veda, a collection of hymns and ritual practices that constitutes the oldest sacred text of Hinduism. For example, one passage refers to an epic clash between a mythic hero, Indra, and a people known as the Dasas:

> He, self-reliant, mighty and triumphant,
>
> brought low the dear head of the wicked Dasas.
>
> Indra the Vritra-slayer, Fort-destroyer,
>
> scattered the Dasa hosts who dwelt in darkness.
>
> For men hath he created earth and waters,
>
> and ever helped the prayer of him who worships.
>
> To him in might the Gods have ever yielded,
>
> to Indra in the tumult of battle.
>
> When in his arms they laid the bolt,
>
> he slaughtered the Dasyus
>
> and cast down their forts of iron.[5]

Against the Aryan Invasion Theory

Not all historians or Hindu scholars agree that the invasion of an ancient nomadic people known as the Aryans lies at the heart of Hinduism's origins. Opponents argue that the "Aryan invasion" theory is based on shaky or nonexistent evidence, and assert that the theory was created by Europeans to falsify and obscure the role of native Indians in the creation of their own religion. In "Demise of the Aryan Invasion Theory," available at www.itihaas.com/ancient/contrib1.html, university professor Dr. Dinesh Agrawal points out that the term Aryan *provided Europeans with a false doctrine of cultural superiority.*

"The most weird aspect of the [Aryan Invasion Theory] is that it has its origin not in any Indian records . . . but in European politics and German nationalism of the 19th century. [It] has no support either in Indian literature, tradition, science, or not even in any of the south Indian (Dravidians, inhabitants of south India, who were supposed to be the victims of the so-called Aryan invasion) literature and tradition. So a product of European politics of the 19th century was forced on Indian history only to serve the imperialist policy of British colonialists to divide the Indian society . . . and accentuate the religious aims of Christian missionaries."

Nevertheless, nearly every textbook, history book, and encyclopedia article dealing with ancient India mentions the Aryan invasion and treats it as established fact. Supporters of the theory point out that Sanskrit is related to languages that later developed in the Middle East and in Europe: the so-called Indo-European tongues. This indicates that the Aryans originated from some point outside of India. They also mention that the term Aryan *appears in the earliest Hindu literature, the Vedas, and is used to designate "one who is respected." At the very least, then, the Aryans were a distinct social class who were considered the "keepers of the flame"—those who maintained the rituals and beliefs of ancient Indian religion. Their origins remain a subject of debate.*

Many scholars believe that this passage is at its heart an account of the invasion of the Indus Valley by the Aryans. It is in the Rig-Veda and three associated Vedas, religious texts that date from around 1500 B.C., that Sanskrit first appears.

About the middle of the second millennium B.C., the Aryan invasion continued to the east and south, conquering the valley of the east-flowing Ganges River and the plains and highlands of what is now central India. Once again, the Aryans' horses and chariots gave them a great advantage in warfare.

According to the Aryan invasion theory, the conquerors had arrived at an opportune time, as the civilization of the Indus Valley was suffering a decline. Once-flourishing cities were being abandoned; crops were failing because of changing climate and soil conditions. The Aryans imposed an entirely new social order on the old society, which gradually disappeared, leaving behind only the ruins of brick cities and a set of beliefs, gods, and ritual practices that would be transformed into a very different religion by the new arrivals.

The Religion of the Aryans

No one is completely certain what beliefs the Aryans brought with them, and what beliefs they adopted from the people they conquered. There are, however, a few clues. For example, some interesting parallels exist between some of the Aryans' beliefs and those of the ancient Europeans. The sky god Dyaus, who is mentioned in the Rig-Veda, may be the same as Zeus, king of the Greek gods. Based on parallels like this, historians speculate that some deities that became members of the Hindu pantheon were already part of Aryan beliefs before the Aryans reached the Indus Valley.

The fertile Indus Valley extends from present-day Pakistan into northwestern India.

The Aryans conducted religious ceremonies around a ritual fire, where the people honored the gods by sacrificing their earthly wealth, such as personal belongings and food. Presiding over the fire sacrifices was a priest, or brahman. The brahman's duty was to carry out rituals in the correct, sanctified manner and to pass on his knowledge of rituals to followers. The ancient Vedas were more than an instruction manual for priests, however. As historian Burton Stein relates in *A History of India*:

> At the core of the Aryan religion was the sacrificial act performed punctiliously by expert brahman priests. . . . But all was not poker-faced austerity and ritual sacrifice, at least not for the gods, seers and rulers depicted in the hymns. Sex, sport, gambling and drinking also figured, and even charitable works. The Asvins, twin horsegods (or horse guards), cured a female seer, Ghosa, of a skin disease that had long rendered her unmarriageable, and went on to provide the son she and her husband could not produce on their own. . . . They rescued shipwrecked sailors and provided a woman warrior with an iron leg when she lost her own in battle.[6]

Over the centuries that followed, the religious practices of the Aryans underwent a transformation as the newcomers adopted some of the forms and beliefs of the people they had conquered. Archaeologists have discovered many ritual baths in the Indus Valley that predate the arrival of the Aryans, who incorporated ritual purification and cleanliness into their own religion. Sacred trees, mountains, rivers, and other places were known to the "pre-Aryans" as well. Some gods and goddesses, such as the elephant-headed god known as Ganesha, are also known to have been worshiped in pre-Aryan India, and were incorporated into the Aryans' Vedic faith—that is, the religion reflected in the text of the Vedas.

The Aryans saw themselves as the chosen people, a noble race whose destiny was to destroy the lowborn natives of India. Their society was as regimented as an army, and by the time of the Rig-Veda was divided into four classes: Brahmans (priests), Kshatriyas (nobles), Vaishyas (farmers), and Sudras (conquered people, servants, slaves). They held horses and cattle in very high esteem, and their favorite occupation was making war. The father was the unquestioned king of his household; sons were expected to assume the occupation of their fathers. Watching over all was Dyaus, the god of the sky; Varuna and Mitra, his sons; and Agni, the god of fire.

At some point, the Aryans began to worship an entirely new deity, a youthful and energetic god of war they knew as Indra. This god was the embodiment of storms and the powerful southwestern monsoon, which he brought to India each year, casting thunder, wind, and heavy rains from his sky-borne chariot. Sinharaja Tammita-Delgoda describes Indra as a

The Aryans worshipped a new deity known as Indra, god of war.

youthful, vigorous hero; given to bragging, drinking and eating huge quantities, his tremendous energy and strength overcame all obstacles. He was the first great leader of the Aryan conquest; heaven and earth are said to have quaked in terror at his birth. . . . It was Indra who defeated the demon Vitra, whose limbless body enveloped the whole world, keeping it in a state of lifelessness and perpetual darkness. Indra destroyed Vitra with his thunderbolt, releasing the sun and the waters, thus bringing life to the earth.[7]

As their Aryan ancestors did, Hindu believers still make offerings to their chosen avatars, or incarnations of God. They leave food or flowers at the base of a statue that lies within a household shrine or at the center of a temple. But in the centuries following the Aryan invasion, the surrender of earthly belongings to a sacrificial fire was replaced by the idea of renunciation—the surrender of material wealth and ordinary pleasures in order to attain enlightenment and serenity. To a Hindu believer, the most sacred life is a life free of striving and free of desire.

The Aryans had among them a group of seers, or *rishis*, who experienced mystical states and visions by drinking a magical elixir known as soma. Historians are not sure of the exact identity of the intoxicating "soma" plant. The secrets of its preparation belonged to members of the priestly class, who pressed the plant, probably a type of milkweed vine, into

Ancient Connections

Historians such as Mark Naidis note a very interesting connection between the gods described in the Vedas and those of the ancient Persians, Greeks, and Hebrews. Naidis draws the following parallels in India: A Short Introductory History.

"Indra rode in his chariot across the sky, leading the Aryan host to destroy the tribal enemy. Indra was associated with storm and thunder and shares much of the character of [the Greek god] Zeus and Thor [the Norse god of thunder]. Vishnu was a sun-god who gained in importance when the Vedic religion was later transmuted into modern Hinduism. Agni was a fire-god who had a special relation with the priest in the horse-sacrifice.... Ethically, the highest of all was Varuna, the guardian of the cosmic order. Like the Hebrew God of the Old Testament, he could visit the sins of the fathers on the sons."

a juice to which was added water, milk, butter, and barley. Soma provided inspiration and visions, allowing the user to gain direct experience of the divine. The visions inspired the writing of holy scriptures that became the fundamental religious literature of modern Hinduism.

The Vedas

The oldest texts of Hinduism, the Vedas, begin with the Rig-Veda, a collection of 1,028 hymns in praise of the ancient gods of the Aryans. The Rig-Veda is both a sacred text and a history lesson. Within its lines, the word *Aryan* appears, meaning "respected" or "high-born," and signifying those who spoke the Sanskrit language and who carried out the rituals designed to preserve the Vedic religion.

The Rig-Veda reveals much about the daily life of the Aryans as they settled in what is now northwestern India. The Rig-Veda's hymns show fathers as priests of their households, and tribal chiefs as the priests of their tribe. They reveal the warlike character of the Aryans, who sometimes fought each other and sometimes fought the darker-skinned natives, whom they considered a lesser race. They also reveal the high status of the priests, who had the secret knowledge that enabled them to conduct sacrifices in the proper way and at the proper time.

The Vedas were preserved as four collections, or Samhitas. Besides the Rig-Veda, the Sama Veda consists of melodies and mantras (chanted phrases) linked with verses of the Rig-Veda. The Yajur Veda collects a series of formulas and incantations to be used by the priest in the Vedic sacrifice. The Atharva Veda, which means "the Veda of the Fire Priest," is a collection of magical incantations and spells, more like folk religion than a description of formal ceremony.

The vast majority of people living in ancient India knew nothing of these works beyond those chants they heard from the lips of the Brahmans, or priests. According to Bruce Sullivan:

> Poems of the Vedic collection were chanted to accompany and make effective the ritual procedures. The rituals, correctly performed, gave the sacrificer access to Brahman, the sacred cosmic power embodied in the ritual and in the Vedic verses. … The gods were invited to attend the ritual, to share in the food, to hear themselves praised for protecting cosmic order and the sacrificer, and were asked in return to aid the sacrificer.[8]

The hymns and mantras of the Rig-Veda describe a sacrificial fire ritual known as *yajnas*. K.M. Sen, in his book *Hinduism*, describes this rite:

> First, yajnas can be looked upon as methods of pleasing gods by giving them parts of one's wealth. Secondly, yajnas can stand for

token offerings made to god to indicate obedience and allegiance. Finally, quite irrespective of the gods, the sacrifices can be looked upon as methods of practising renunciation.[9]

Like much ancient sacred literature, the Rig-Veda proclaims its beliefs with certainty, imparting to the reader the key to secret knowledge and practices known to few. But the Rig-Veda also expresses something almost unknown in the literature of other religions: doubt over the true origins of the world and of mankind. One Vedic verse known as the "Hymn of Creation" suggests what may be unknowable:

Brahma is the Hindu god of creation.

Darkness was hidden by darkness in the beginning; with no distinguishing signs, all this was water. The life-force was covered in emptiness . . . arose through the power of heat.

Who really knows? Who will here proclaim it? Whence was it produced? Whence was this creation? The gods came afterwards, with the creation of this universe. Who then really knows whence it has arisen?

Whence this creation has arisen— perhaps it formed itself, or perhaps it did not—the one who looks down on it, in the highest heaven, only he knows—or perhaps he does not know.[10]

Later Vedic Sacred Works

The oldest four collections of the Vedas—the Samhitas—are at least three thousand years old. But the creation of the sacred texts of Hinduism did not end with the Samhitas. As the native people of the Indus Valley and northern India began to mingle and intermarry with the Aryan invaders, and as their religions and culture also began to mix, new ideas emerged. Over the centuries, the priests saw their rituals and their beliefs challenged.

Much of this challenge and change is expressed in the collected texts known

as the Brahmanas, the Aranyakas, and the Upanishads. The Brahmanas are commentaries on the meaning of sacrifice, the most important ritual of ancient India. These texts lay out very detailed and precise instructions on how to make sacrifices and, as their title suggests, are meant for the use of Vedic priests, not for popular consumption. Certainly, to a modern reader, and even to a modern Hindu, they can seem very strange and obscure. As scholar D.J. Melling admits:

> The rites discussed in the Brahmanas are ancient and very complicated, and even a reader with a committed interest in religion and theology is unlikely to be gripped by a nine-chapter-long discussion of the exact placing of bricks in the building of a fire altar or by the prescription for the proper use of horse-dung in ritual fumigation.[11]

The Aranyakas were set down at about the same time as the Brahmanas, from about 900 to 700 B.C. They are also known as "forest texts," as they represent conversations and debates held by sages and seekers while wandering in a forest. Instead of setting down the rules and instructions for the outward performance of sacrifice, however, the speakers debate its meaning.

The Upanishads

While the Brahmanas and the Aranyakas deal with how sacrifice should
be conducted and what it means, the
third text, the Upanishads, shows how
sacrifice affects the relationship between
gods and humans. The Upanishads are
written in the form of lessons or explanations given by gurus (teachers) to
their students. The name means "to sit
down near"; the Upanishads describe a
lesson given at the feet of a master.

These texts contain secret or mystical
knowledge that is known only to certain
adepts (those trained in the Vedic religion). Developed by many different
philosophers, the Upanishads can be
dated over several centuries, beginning
around 800 B.C. According to one
Hindu tradition, there are 108 Upanishads, but not all are given equal weight
by Hindu scholars. Some claim that
only 13 Upanishads represent authentic
Vedic literature, while only 15 were considered "major" Upanishads by the
philosopher Shankara, a religious authority who lived in the ninth century A.D.
Religious and philosophical writings
known as "Upanishads" have been written throughout history, and some even
date to modern times.

The significance of the ancient
Upanishads lies in their description of
a religious revolution in the making.
Previously the Vedic gods and spirits
had stood unchallenged, but now their
authority and position were usurped
by a single, all-pervading spirit known
as Brahman, which can be expressed
within each individual soul, or atman.
As the Brahman merges with the
atman, the ancient and powerful class
of sacrificial priests loses its place to the
faith and knowledge of the individual,
humble believer.

The Upanishads, which likely were
the work of Indian mystics, describe a
belief in transmigration, or the journey
of the soul after death. According to
historian Mark Naidis:

> The souls of people who lived lives
> of sacrifice, charity, and austerity
> went into space, then passed into the
> air and descended to the earth as rain.
> Rain was absorbed into plants, which
> were eaten by women. Concep-
> tion then occurred through the eating
> of a fruit or vegetable. The idea of
> rebirth seems to have gained ground
> in the seventh and sixth centuries
> B.C.[12]

So in the Upanishads ancient writers
began describing and defining reincarnation. At the same time they developed the concept of karma. This idea is
easy to understand: Karma is the result
of actions undertaken during a single
lifetime. It may lead one to reincarnation in another life, either more developed or less, depending on the nature of

these actions. It may also lead to freedom from the cycle of reincarnation—the desired result. Freedom from reincarnation can be attained through knowledge: the realization that the soul (atman) and the sacred cosmic power (Brahman) are one and the same.

The many gods identified and described in the Vedas and which became part of Hindu belief include deities associated with the sun, the moon, the dawn, the sky, fire, rain, water, and other natural forces. In addition, there are the opposing groups of Devas and Asuras—as some historians call them, gods and demons. These two groups fight an epic war to dominate the world, a fight eventually won by the Devas, who set down the system that made human society possible.

Though the body of Vedic literature ends with the Upanishads, the sacred texts of Hinduism would grow in the centuries to come, in the form of epics that describe the action of the Hindu gods and their avatars, or representatives on earth. Instead of chants, prayers, ritual formulas, and the like, the epics describe actions in a more familiar world, the world of fighting and action, jealousy and greed, and ordinary human traits and foibles. Some scholars, in fact, see these newer writings as describing an entirely different religion and continuing a vigorous debate over the ideas and very definition of the faith. While they call the religion of the Vedas and the Upanishads "Brahmanism" or "Vedism," the epics describe what they see as true "Hinduism."

chapter | two

The Hindu Gods and Epics

The Vedas, the Brahmanas, the Aranyakas, and the Upanishads make up only the beginnings of Hindu literature. Hindus refer to these works as shruti texts, or "heard" texts, meaning they were received directly from a divine source by priests who in turn passed them down orally to their students. The shruti texts include beliefs held by both the Aryans and the original inhabitants of the Indus Valley, known to historians simply as the "pre-Aryans."

By the time the religion of the Aryans (known as the Vedic religion because so much of it is contained in the Vedas) had become well established in northern India, new works describing Hindu gods and heroes were being written. These are known as smriti texts, which are "remembered" by their authors as legendary exploits of the distant past. The earliest parts of the *Mahabharata*, the best known of these works, date from around the third or second century B.C. This "Epic of the War of the Bharatas," is written in Sanskrit, the language that developed among the priests and highest strata of society. The *Mahabharata* is the longest poem ever written, comprising ninety thousand couplets, or double verses. According to tradition, the poem was written by a sage named Vyasa, but historians believe that the *Mahabharata* is actually the work of many writers and poets whose works were set down over a period of six hundred years.

The *Mahabharata* describes a war between two rival clans, the Kauravas and the Pandavas. But the *Mahabharata* is much more than a military epic. It includes long passages about the origin of the world, the nature of the Hindu gods, and the duty of humans in service to these gods. The central story describes Lord Arjuna, a member of the Pandava clan, and his chariot driver, Lord Krishna. Historians believe that this section may actually represent the conquest of northern India by the Aryan tribes, who had arrived at least a thousand years earlier. According to authors Bridget and Raymond Allchin, others point to a war known to have been fought between the Bharatas and a confederacy of ten other Aryan tribes: "The leader of the Bharatas at that time was Sudas, and the 'Battle of the Ten Kings' became a subject of heroic record which has sometimes been supposed to have provided one of the sources for the later epic story of the *Mahabharata*."[13]

Alongside the narrative of this epic conflict, the *Mahabharata* lays down the

Motorists ride past cattle in the streets of New Dehli, India. To a Hindu, the sacredness of a cow is more important than the inconvenience of a traffic jam.

The Sacred Syllable

Since the creation of the Upanishads, Hindus have held a single vocalized syllable in great reverence: Om. This sound is said to be the basis of all mantras and hymns sung by Hindu believers. It was the sound by which the world was created, and the sound to which the world will end.

The sound of Om is said to have good effects on the psyche and on the body. It is a memory aid believed to help a student of Hinduism remember each lesson if it is chanted at the beginning and the end of the lesson. It protects those making sacrifices from any errors, and provides good fortune in general.

law of correct living and duty among Hindu believers. It also describes the division of Hindu society into separate castes, a division that would endure for thousands of years. According to scholar Louis Renou:

Brahma . . . formed truth, righteousness, austere fervor, and the eternal Veda, virtuous practice, and purity for the attainment of heaven. He also formed the gods, demons, and men, Brahmins, Kshatriyas, Vaishyas. Those Brahmins, who derived their livelihood from kine [cattle], who were yellow, who subsisted by agriculture, and who neglected to practice their duties, entered into the state of Vaishyas. Those Brahmins, who were addicted to mischief and falsehood, who were covetous, who lived by all kinds of work, who were black and had fallen from

purity, sank into the condition of Sudras.[14]

In accordance with this passage of the *Mahabharata,* four main castes came to be recognized: Brahmans are priests and teachers; Kshatriyas are warriors and administrators; Vaishyas are merchants, farmers, and traders; Sudras represent those who undertake all kinds of physical labor. Specific colors were associated with each caste: Brahmans, white; Kshatriyas, red; Vaishyas, yellow; Sudras, black.

The *Mahabharata* treats hundreds of religious concepts and practices, and more than two thousand years later, millions of Hindus would continue to apply its precepts to the conduct of their daily lives. The sacred status of cows, for example, has one of its most eloquent explanations in the lines of the *Mahabharata:*

No sacrifice can be performed without the aid of curds and ghee [clarified butter]. The very character of sacrifice which sacrifices have, depends upon ghee. Hence ghee (or, the cow from which it is produced) is regarded as the very root of sacrifice.

Cows have been said to be the limbs of sacrifice. They represent sacrifice itself. Without them, there can be no sacrifice....

Of all kinds of gifts, the gift of cows is applauded as the highest. Cows are the foremost of all things. Themselves sacred, they are the best of cleansers and sanctifiers. People should cherish cows for obtaining prosperity and even peace. Cows are said to represent the highest energy both in this world and the world that is above.

There is nothing that is more sacred or sanctifying than cows.[15]

The sacredness of cows came from their importance in the daily lives of the Aryans, who saw their herds as the most important thing they owned. Sinharaja Tammita-Delgoda explains: "Cattle were the most important source of wealth and served as a sort of currency. The farmer prayed for an increase in cattle, the warrior expected cattle as booty and the priest was rewarded for his services with cattle."[16]

The importance of cattle was reflected in the fact that those who had to slaughter them, and who had to work their skins into leather, were considered unclean and "untouchable." From that time forward, leatherworking would be considered an unclean occupation, to be per-

The Sacred Cow

Cows remain sacred creatures within India today. No Hindu believer will knowingly harm a cow, and millions of the animals roam free on the streets of Hindu villages in India. The sacredness of cows is at the root of Hindu vegetarianism. While some Hindus are strictly vegetarian and eat no meat whatsoever, some eat chicken or fish as often as they please, but never beef.

Leather produced from the hide of a cow is also considered ritually impure among Hindus. Traditionally, leatherworkers are considered without caste or "untouchable." As impure objects, leather shoes and sandals are not worn in the home, or in certain sanctified areas of the home. Shoes are always removed on entering a temple.

formed only by "outcaste" members of Indian society, and the cow would be considered a sacred animal by Hindus everywhere.

The Bhagavad Gita

For its direct and easily understood moral teachings, one seven-hundred-verse section of the *Mahabharata* achieved great popularity among Hindu scholars and students and enduring sacred and literary value. The Bhagavad Gita describes the teachings of Krishna, the charioteer of Lord Arjuna. Krishna, an incarnation of the god Vishnu, advises Lord Arjuna, who is experiencing the fear and doubt of warfare on the battle-field.

Although Arjuna wishes to avoid fighting this battle, Krishna instructs him that it is his duty to carry on, as that is Arjuna's dharma—his religious duty as a member of the Kshatriyas, or class of warriors. Arjuna is predestined to do battle; in the same way, it is only right for the members of any caste to live and worship as it is ordained for their caste.

As quoted in the Bhagavad Gita, Krishna says, "Better to do one's own caste duty, though devoid of merit, than to do another's however well performed. By doing the works prescribed by his own nature a man meets no defilement."[17]

The lesson of the Bhagavad Gita became the central precept of Hinduism as it was practiced in later ages, and as it is known in the present day. In Hindu thought, living the right way, according to an individual's duties, or dharma, should be the believer's ultimate goal. Every action that a person takes results in a force, or karma, which can be good or bad according to the nature of the action. Karma is produced by everything one does, down to the smallest thought or unconscious action, such as breathing.

The sum total of karma over a single lifetime results in the incarnation, good or bad, that the soul achieves in the next life it experiences. Some actions will produce good karma, which everyone aspires to. These include meditation, knowledge, selfless actions, and surrender to God. Following the duties of dharma, and attaining good karma, means liberating the soul from the endless cycle of reincarnation (samsara), in which the soul dies only to be reborn again on earth in another form. This liberation, known as moksha, means losing all of life's ordinary troubles, needs, and desires, and finally attaining paradise.

The *Ramayana*

In part, the *Mahabharata* instructs the faithful through the examples set by Krishna and Arjuna. Another important epic, the *Ramayana*, instructs through the actions of a mighty king, Rama, and his efforts to recapture his wife, Sita, who is kidnapped by Ravana, the king of Lanka (modern Sri Lanka, a large island off the southeastern tip of India). While the *Mahabharata* may be a reflection of the Aryan invasions of the north, scholars believe the *Ramayana* describes the gradual spread of northern Indian institutions and culture to the south.

Both the *Mahabharata* and the *Ramayana* include hundreds of tales, told by the main characters, as well as religious teachings and moral instruction. Both Lord Krishna and Rama represent divinities who have come down to earth to interact with ordinary human beings. Gradually, the Hindu religion accepted such avatars, or earthly manifestations, who gained popularity among common people who had little knowledge of the philosophies and practices of the priestly caste as described in the Vedas.

Over the centuries, the various heroes of the Hindu epics would provide models for the behavior of Hindu believers, as author K.M. Sen relates:

The honesty, sincerity, and love of his fellow creatures that we find in Rama, the chastity and kindness of Sita, the brotherly affection of

Lakshmana and Bharata have been archetypes of conduct for many generations. Similarly, in the Mahabharata, the self-sacrifice of Bhisma, the truthfulness and forgiveness of Yudhisthira, the love of justice and the desire to protect the weak from the strong of the Pandava brothers, and the generosity of Karna on the side of the Kurus have provided ideals to countless Indians for many generations.[18]

The Trimurti

The sacred works of Hinduism portray many deities. But three of these gods (the trimurti) rose to hold a leading place in the Hindu pantheon. These three gods are Brahma, Vishnu, and Shiva. Put as simply as possible, Brahma is the creator, Vishnu the preserver, and Shiva the destroyer and regenerator of all things. Brahma is the deity that balances Vishnu and Shiva, the preserving and destroying forces. Brahma is the personification of Brahman, the sacred power that underlies all existence. He also represents the balancing of the opposing forces of Vishnu and Shiva. Karel Werner, in *A Popular Dictionary of Hinduism*, describes Brahma's elusive nature:

Reduced to playing an active part only at the beginning of the world cycle, he is often thought of as sunk in cosmic slumber or deep meditation and has to be awakened if he is needed. He is depicted with four heads, bearded, and with four arms. His wife is Sarasvati, originally his daughter, and his mount is the goose or swan. He has only two temples dedicated to him in India.[19]

Historians believe that Brahma was introduced by the priests and scholars of India after the time of the Vedic texts, in an effort to balance the rival cults of Shiva and Vishnu. The addition of Brahma to the pantheon was perhaps a natural part of the evolution of Hindu belief. Established gods and spirits gradually faded away from once-vaunted places in the Hindu pantheon. Others were transformed, acquiring new names and aspects. The principal Hindu gods have collected many different names, and absorbed many other gods as their avatars.

Each deity has his or her following of devotees. For example, one

The protector and preserver god Vishnu, and the goddess Lakshmi, ride the mythical birdlike creature Garuda.

family may worship Vishnu, or an avatar of Vishnu—they are Vaishnavites. Another pays little attention to him and follows Shiva—they are Shivaites. Neither family considers that they have found the true or most authentic form of Hinduism. While they do hold some basic beliefs in common, Hindus recognize that there are as many different ways to worship and practice their faith as there are believers.

This endless transformation and permutation of the Hindu gods has brought Vishnu to a prominent place among Hindus in modern times. Those who follow Vishnu also know this god as Narayana, meaning "the all pervading." They consider Vishnu the ultimate builder and preserver of the world. From time to time, he came down to earth in the form of an avatar, and the stories of the deeds of these avatars—such as Rama and Krishna— are told in a number of sacred texts. Among Hindus, Siddhartha Gautama, the founder of Buddhism, is considered to be another of Vishnu's avatars.

Historian Burton Stein describes the history of Vishnu:

A Reason for Lord Rama

Where do the gods of any religion originate? One possibility is that they represent basic elements worshiped by ancient humans, who lived completely at the mercy of natural forces. Writer Sudheer Birodkar, in his book Hindu History, *available online at www.hindubooks.org/sudheer_birodkar/hindu_history/contents.html, points out the possible origins of Lord Rama in the worship of light and the sun.*

"There is some link between Lord Rama and Sun Worship. The Sun is considered to be the progenitor of Rama's dynasty which is called the Sun dynasty. . . . Rama is also known as Raghunatha, Raghupati, Raghavendra, etc. That all these names begin with the prefix Raghu is also suggestive of some link with Sun-worship. The hour chosen for the observance of the lord's birth is that when the sun is overhead and is at its maximum brilliance. Significantly, the ancient Egyptians termed the sun as Amon Ra or simply as "Ra." In Latin the syllable Ra is used to connote light. For example, we have Radiance which [means] emission of light, or Radium which means any substance emitting light or brilliance. The common element is the syllable Ra, which in many languages is used to derive words describing Sun or light."

Vishnu was elaborated by . . . a range of god-figures, including a boar, whose primitive worship was popular in western India, and, at the other extreme, Rama, the perfect king of the Ramayana. The boar—the divine Veraha—and Rama joined other assimilated deities as avatars, the manifestations in which Vishnu came among mankind to save it from demons. The entire panoply then constituted a pantheon of gods whose worship was equivalent to devotion to Vishnu.[20]

Modern artists depict Vishnu with a bluish face and with four hands, which hold a lotus, a mace, a conch, and a discus. The god floats on a pool, symbolizing unmanifest reality; the lotus that grows from his navel symbolizes his creativity. In Hindu mythology, according to Werner,

Vishnu moves about riding on his mount Garuda, a mythical bird-like creature, sometimes portrayed as half-human. . . . At the end of the world period he brings about the emanation from his forehead of Shiva, who then destroys the universe by means of his cosmic dance. After Vishnu has had a period of rest on his snake couch, during which he is united with the goddess Yoganidra, the process of creation starts all over again.[21]

Shiva

While Vishnu represents the forces of protection and preservation, Shiva represents the opposite forces of destruction and regeneration. Long before the Aryans arrived, Shiva was worshiped by the Indus Valley people as the god of storms. Gradually, the believers in the Vedic religion incorporated this storm god into their own beliefs.

To non-Hindus, Shiva's character may seem hard to describe. Kanitkar and Cole explain:

Shiva worship combines many contradictory elements: fear, uncertainty of the unknown, regeneration, powers of death and destruction, mystic forces of human psyche and malignant aspects of nature. . . . He is associated with evil and cruel spirits, ghosts, goblins, and vampires, which haunt funeral grounds. He is believed to have a third eye in the middle of his forehead, with which he destroyed the god of love.[22]

One of the most familiar images of Hinduism is the dancing Shiva, a statue in which a four-armed god is

Shiva represents the forces of destruction and regeneration.

shown dancing within a circle of flames. Through its many visual clues, the statue holds an entire lesson on the meaning of Shiva. The god carefully balances on one leg atop a dwarf, with one right hand holding a drum. The drum symbolizes the creation of the world, which occurs to a constant and eternal rhythm. One of the left hands holds a flame, which brings about the constant destruction of the physical world. The second right hand is held up to assure the viewer that the cycle of creation and destruction is eternal, like a dance that does not end.

The second left hand? Joseph Campbell explains:

The second left hand of the god Shiva is held out before him in what is called the elephant posture.... This is the teaching hand. This elephant or teaching hand points to the left foot, which is lifted; and that lift signifies release. Meanwhile, however, the right foot is driving down into the back of the dwarf, whose name is "Ignorance." This foot is driving souls into ignorance—that is to say, into the world, into creation, into this life that we are leading. But the other foot is lifting, yielding release.[23]

Shiva is also known as Bhairava, the Terrible; Vishvanath, the Lord of the Universe; and Nataraja, the God of Dancing, among many other names. In fact, Shiva is said to have 1,008 different names altogether, each of which describes a different aspect of his character. As Dolf Hartsuiker explains in *Sadhus: India's Mystic Holy Men:*

Eventually [Shiva] was elevated to the highest position in the Hindu pantheon, forming part of the trinity Brahma-Vishnu-Shiva as the god of Destruction. He is not a brutal annihilator, but, like a forest fire preparing the ground for new vegetation, he destroys and re-creates, as these two life processes are inseparable and complementary. In this "terrible" aspect he is Hara, the "seizer," representing death and sleep; and he is Mahakala, the Great Timekeeper, calculating the aeons and leading all things to final dissolution.[24]

A cult devoted to Shiva gradually gained strength in ancient India; followers performed sacrifices to images of the god. These ceremonies probably took place inside public temples, but historians know little about what these places looked like, as they were all made of wood, and none have survived into modern times.

In its tales and myths, the Vedic religion explained earthly occurrences as the result of actions among the gods. In this way, acts of a moral nature—heroism or cowardice, charity and faithfulness—were transformed into legendary acts of the gods. Old wars between the Aryans and non-Aryans, and among the various Aryan tribes, were preserved in memory as epic battles among the avatars. The nineteenth-century French missionary J.A. Dubois might have been describing one such transformation in a tale surrounding the god Shiva:

In one of his wars, wishing by an unexpected attack to accomplish

the ruin of all his enemies, the giants. . . . He split the earth into two equal parts, and took one-half as a weapon. He made Brahma the general of his army; the four Vedas served him for horses. Vishnu was used as an arrow, while Mandra Parvata served as a bow. In place of a bow-string he tied to his bow a monstrous serpent. With this formidable equipment Shiva led his army against the enemies of the gods, took from them the three fortresses which they had constructed, and exterminated them all without sparing a single one.[25]

Together, Vishnu and Shiva form a sort of opposing pair, each balancing the style and characteristics of the other. As Hartsuiker explains:

The world of Vishnu contrasts with Shiva's as day and night. At the same time they form a complementary whole, the Yin and Yang—to borrow a foreign concept—of Hinduism: Shiva the moon-god, the aloof ascetic, alone in the heart of the infinite; and Vishnu the sun-god, merciful warrior-king, the close friend of mankind who descends to earth whenever the world has to be saved from doom.[26]

Besides the trimurti, a number of other deities are widely recognized. One of these is Kali, a malignant goddess of uncontrolled energy. Kali represents humankind's worst nightmare, one that must be faced squarely in order to be calmed. Margaret and James Stutley describe her terrifying appearance:

> Kali symbolizes eternal time and hence she both gives life and destroys it. Her appearance is described as a hideous four-armed emaciated woman with fang-like teeth, who devours all beings. She holds a pasa (noose), khatvanga (skull-topped staff), khadga (sword) and a severed head. The weapons denote her powers of destruction; the severed head, that there is no escape from time, and that individual lives and deaths are merely minute episodes in the time Continuum.[27]

Kali also has black skin, a color that signifies an end to all differences as well as nighttime, the period that precedes creation. In some representations, she stands atop the corpse of Shiva.

The Crowded Hindu Pantheon

Hinduism has room for many more deities, a fact that has led many people to believe that it is not a monotheistic (one-god) religion. Hindus see things differently. In Hindu practice, the various gods and goddesses are simply different manifestations of God (sometimes known as Brahman), an all-pervading deity that exists both in the material world and on a divine, transcendent plane, and which has taken many forms through the ages.

The Rig-Veda, the oldest sacred text of Hinduism, gives praise to many different deities, representing creation's many different aspects and forces, as Kanitkar and Cole note,

Kali's frightful appearance greets visitors at a roadside shrine.

The chief among them being: Aditi, the mother, and the Adityas, the deities of light (including Vishnu); Agni, god of fire, Aryaman, god of ancestors; Dyaus, god of the sky; Maruts, the storm deities, Rudra being the chief among them: Mitra and Surya (the Sun), deities of light; Panjanya, god of rain; Prithvi, goddess of earth; Ushas, goddess of the dawn; Varuna, god of water; Vayu, the wind god; and Yama, god of death.[28]

A few of these gods survive relatively unchanged, a few others have been transformed, and a few have been forgotten. Each has his or her following. But one of the most popular gods among Hindus everywhere is Ganesha, the adopted son of Shiva. Ganesha is easy to recognize, as he is always shown with the head of an elephant. This god who reflects the veneration of elephants in pre-Aryan India, represents wisdom, learning, and good fortune. When faced with one of life's problems, with a difficult test, or with a long journey, a Hindu turns to Ganesha for assistance and a bit of luck. But the origins of this god were anything but happy or lucky. One day, according to the Ganesha legend, Parvati, the wife of Shiva, made a clay statue of a boy and breathed life into it

Ganesha, the god with the elephant head, is one of India's most popular deities.

to create a son and a guardian of the house. When Shiva unexpectedly arrived home, he discovered the boy and, in a towering rage, cut off his head. When Parvati arrived at the scene and discovered the corpse, she explained to Shiva that he had just killed their only son. The remorseful Shiva then promised to have the head replaced—as the god of destruction and regeneration, he was well suited to the job. He sent out his servants to find the head of someone—anyone—who happened to be asleep and whose head faced north. The servants searched for a long time, and finally found a young elephant that fit Shiva's description. The head was brought back and Shiva rebuilt his son, naming him Ganesha, or lord of the attendants.

Ganesha always appears with his elephant's head, but also with just one tusk. A rat stands nearby, attending the god and serving as his mount. Ganesha holds in his hands a snare, an ax, and sweets. With his free hand, Ganesha offers a blessing to those who recognize and worship him.

Another figure that has been venerated by Hindus is Lord Krishna, the eighth avatar of Vishnu. Traditionally, Krishna is said to have been born of royalty, but was raised by Nanda, a herdsman, and his wife Yasoa because his mother feared that the evil King Kamsa was planning to kill him. Krishna spent a pleasant boyhood and gained a reputation as a prankster, seducer, and skilled flute player. His great courage allowed Krishna to become an accomplished warrior and slay many demons and dragons. On the instructions he received from Vishnu in a vision, Krishna carried out his most heroic act in the killing of the tyrannical King Kamsa.

In the *Mahabharata*, Krishna is portrayed as taking a divine form and fighting on the side of the Pandava family against the Kauravas. It is Krishna who speaks out for duty and honor in the Bhagavad Gita, in which

A boy dressed as Krishna is carried above the crowd in a procession celebrating the birthday of Krishna.

he gives profound advice on dharma and the fulfillment of destiny to the troubled hero Arjuna. In the Bhagavad Gita, he also promises to return whenever religion is troubled on earth: "Whenever and wherever there is a decline in religious practice, O descendant of Bharata, and a predominant rise of irreligion at that time I descend Myself. To deliver the pious and to annihilate the miscreants, as well as to reestablish the principles of religion, I Myself appear millenium after millenium."[29]

Hindu artists portray Krishna with a blue face and often depict him as a young boy with a flute in his hands. Writers believe he might have been one of the non-Aryan heroes adopted into the pantheon of Vedic gods brought by the Aryan invaders. In modern India, Krishna remains one of the most beloved of all incarnations of Vishnu, a symbol of divinity, courage, and hope. Krishna's story also represents the diffusion of the secret priestly knowledge to the mass of common people, who heard in this god's words ancient wisdom and ideas in terms that they could understand.

chapter | three

The Spread and Development of Hinduism

As Hindu philosophies spread to the mass of ordinary people in India, secret knowledge that had once belonged only to members of a priestly caste began to change. The faith that one day would be called Hinduism began touching on many aspects of daily living, and on the proper ways to carry out one's duties to the family and community.

Certain ideas came to be shared by all believers, no matter where they lived or what class they belonged to. One of these was the belief in the process of reincarnation, or the rebirth of the soul after death, and the ultimate goal of the faithful in moksha, or liberation from this process. The people of India also began to accept the idea of karma: Certain actions, no matter how involuntary or insignificant, have consequences for the soul and for the prospects of future reincarnations.

The Purusharthas of Life

The question, then, is how one goes about improving one's prospects. Hindu philosophers hold that there are four important moral aspects or qualities, known as purusharthas, to which every man and woman must strive. The first of these is dharma, right practice and beliefs that preserve the faith and maintain the individual, the family, and the society in equilibrium. For Hindus, following one's dharma means carrying out those practices that keep him or her "right with God." This can mean the strict observance of daily rituals, or the visit to a temple each week. It can also mean correctly observing dietary restrictions, the method of praying and making sacrifices, or more generally the treatment of others. Dharma also means the proper way of going in pursuit of two other qualities: artha and kama.

Artha signifies prosperity, wealth, and material possessions. It includes the performance of one's job, or the pursuit of trade; it also means providing for one's family and for the community at large. Kama is physical sensation and pleasure; it signifies such bodily drives and impulses as hunger, excitement, sex, and laughter. A Hindu seeks to keep artha and kama in balance, to not indulge one by sacrificing the other, and to keep his or her dharma always uppermost in mind. The writer Pandharinath Prabhu explains that "by attending to his dharma, therefore, a person is able to live a proper life even though it may be lived in terms of artha and kama."[30]

A weekly visit to the temple is one of those practices that keeps a Hindu "right with God."

The fourth quality, moksha, signifies inner spiritual life, which in its highest form culminates in liberation from reincarnation. More generally, it is the drive for spiritual perfection and the realization of divinity in oneself. Whereas dharma concerns how one deals with the world outside, moksha is the inner world and the effect one's personal beliefs, observations, dreams, opinions, and so on have on oneself. Prabhu writes:

> [Moksha] refers, perhaps, to the appeal of the inner man to the individual, unaffected by the group. It is perhaps too personal an outlook that defines the struggle and hope and justification within the individual for moksha. But, from the Hindu's point of view, we must also remember that the inner personality of the individual, at its best, is identified by him not only with the group, nor only with society, nor with the nation, nor the race, nor even with the entire human race, but with the whole creation, animate and inanimate, seen and unseen, which includes all these.[31]

Over the centuries, Hinduism developed many different ways of perceiving the world and the life of the individual. But in contrast to other major religions, Hinduism is more a system of action than a system of belief. So regardless of beliefs regarding specific deities, the man or woman who practices his or her dharma, and who follows a path meant to lead to enlightenment, is a Hindu. Since the time of the earliest Vedic religion—that is, the faith brought to India by Aryan invaders—guidance on this path has been provided by scholars, teachers, and philosophers, who took their inspiration from those who had lived before them, and who eventually brought Hinduism to every region of India and even beyond India's long frontiers.

Spreading the Faith

At the time the Hindu epics were first being set down, the common people knew the Vedas and the epics only through the stories told and mantras chanted by the priests. They also learned by listening to bhajans, poems of devotion set down by authors in local languages such as Gujarati and Marathi.

In the centuries after they were written down and collected, the epics of Hinduism were translated from Sanskrit, their original language, into the other languages of the Indian subcontinent. This helped spread the faith into southern and eastern India, and eventually to the island of Sri Lanka, lying off the southeastern coast of the Indian subcontinent. As a new group or culture adopted the faith, each added its own particular ideas or interpretations.

Epics such as the *Mahabharata* and the *Ramayana* served to entertain listeners and readers and to teach the fruits of right thought and right action. As told in *Voices from India*, the same is true even in modern times:

> Almost no Indian does not know the stories from the Ramayana— as told by Vlamiki many centuries ago and retold in endless variations. The epic recounts Rama's exile, the faithfulness of his wife Sita and brother Lakshman in accompanying him, the abduction of Sita by Lanka the demon king of Ceylon, Rama's rescue of Sita with the help of the monkey king Hanuman, and Rama's return to his kingdom. Similarly, everyone is brought up in home, village, and school to legends from the Mahabharata.[32]

The Cults of Devotion

Hinduism underwent significant changes around the fourth century A.D., when the Gupta Empire arose. The Gupta rulers were natives of India who held sway in the northern half of the country. This was a time when India enjoyed considerable

Young people study the epic stories of the Hindu faith.

prosperity. The Guptas raised magnificent cities and presided over a renaissance of art and culture. They also adopted new religious icons and practices. Most importantly, Tammita-Delgoda notes, during the Gupta period Hindus began to worship images of the gods:

> The temple started to become the focus of social and religious life and it was during this period that images began to be worshipped.

The Fraternity of Stranglers

Hinduism has given rise to many different brotherhoods, associations, and cults whose practices seem more or less peculiar to outside observers. In northern and central India, however, a fraternity arose whose practices proved too outrageous for even the most tolerant outsiders. The "Thugs" dedicated themselves to the goddess Bhavani, a form of Kali, the goddess of destruction. Their faith required robbing adult males and strangling them with a rope. Margaret and James Stutley, in Harper's Dictionary of Hinduism, *give the gory details:*

"Some of the Thugs concentrated their activities in the Ganges area between Banares and Calcutta, plying boats with crews of fifteen, ostensibly to convey pilgrims, whom they flung into the river after robbing them. Others roamed about the country in small bands or joined up with travellers whose confidence they had gained.

Of the various methods adopted by the Thugs to dispatch their victims garrotting [strangling] was the more usual, but none of their methods involved the shedding of blood. The victims were buried in a hole dug with a sacred pickaxe, an implement greatly venerated and worshipped by Thugs, and upon which oaths were sworn, and by which they practised divination."

The British colonizers of India undertook a very long campaign to rid the country of the Thugs. By the 1860s, according to the Stutleys, the Thugs were driven out of settled areas of India.

There was also an upsurge in the popular worship of Shiva and Vishnu, who now overshadowed the other gods in the Hindu pantheon. As a result, Hinduism itself assumed a new form and began to divide into two main sects—the Vaishnavites, the worshippers of Vishnu, and the Shivaites, the worshippers of Shiva.[33]

Rather than fragile wood, the new temples were constructed of brick or stone. They housed an image of the god, which was placed in the center of the building. Devotees would enter the temples through a small veranda, and walk a circular path around the image after entering.

Royalty of the Gupta period saw the temples as symbols of their power and achievements. The temples were marked with religious inscriptions and decorated with sculpture, all to glorify the devotion and piety of the ruler who commissioned and supported them. To increase their standing among the people and in the eyes of the gods, the kings also rewarded Brahmans with land and property.

Another change was the way in which Hindus related to their deities. The cults of Shiva and Vishnu based themselves not on sacred, secret knowledge but on personal devotion, or bhakti. The knowledge of bhakti was conveyed not through books of hymns and rituals, heard directly by a high-caste priest from a divine source, but through the Puranas, books of Sanskrit verse that date from the fourth century A.D. These collections of legends and myths could be heard, read, and understood by ordinary people. Each of the eighteen major Puranas also deals with a god, his or her place in the pantheon of Hindu gods, and the proper understanding and worship of that god. In fact, it was in the Puranas that the trimurti of Brahma, Vishnu, and Shiva became the three most important aspects or manifestations of God.

One Purana describes the truly devoted followers of Vishnu in straightforward yet poetic language:

Know that excellent man to be a worshipper of Vishnu, who, looking upon gold in secret, holds that which is another's wealth but as grass, and devotes all his thoughts

to the lord. Pure is he as a mountain of clear crystal; for how can Vishnu abide in the hearts of men with malice, and envy, and other evil passions? The flowing heat of fire abides not in a cluster of the cooling rays of the moon. He who lives pure in thought, free from malice, contented, leading a holy life, feeling tenderness for all creatures, speaking wisely and kindly, humble and sincere, has Vasudeva [Vishnu] ever present in his heart.[34]

The Hindu temple is the center of religious and social life.

Such writing made a very clear and moving appeal to ordinary people, who no longer had to struggle to understand the obscure hymns and prayers of a priestly caste. The bhakti cults made the ancient Vedic gods and spirits, and the gods who rose to importance long after Vedic religion began, personal and realistic—almost human. The believer felt an intense and very personal joy in the presence of the god—a feeling more like love for a friend or a relative than awe for a distant deity that cannot be seen or easily understood. The bhakti cults had important effects on the culture of India. They inspired devotional poetry, music, and art that became classics.

But violence and bitter rivalry also emerged during this period. Many of the kings who adopted the beliefs of the bhakti cults campaigned against rival sects, particularly against Buddhism, which had arisen as an offshoot of Hinduism. There was no doctrine of nonviolence working among these rulers. Their campaigns resulted in killings and the destruction of Buddhist monasteries. Many Buddhist shrines, including a shrine built at the site where Buddha himself was supposed to have achieved his enlightenment, were forcefully returned to the Hindu gods.

The Hindu Schools

Like all major religions, Hinduism developed separate schools of thought, taught by gurus who identified themselves with one or more of its philosophies. Over the course of more than two thousand years, six orthodox schools of Hindu philosophy developed: Nyaya, Vaiseshika, Puva-Mimamsa, Vedanta, Samkhya, and Yoga. In Hinduism, *writer K.M. Sen explains:*

"The Nyaya deals mainly with logical methods and the Vaiseshika mainly with the nature of the world. . . . The Puva-Mimamsa . . . is interested mainly in inquiring into the nature of dharma (right action)."

The Vedanta is a school of philosophy based on the knowledge and interpretation of the Vedas. The most famous Vedanta teacher, Shankara, was born in A.D. 788. Although he died at the young age of thirty-two, Shankara founded four philosophical colleges that still exist in modern India. He taught that everything a person perceives in the world is an illusion, that the only real phenomenon is the all-pervading force known as the Brahman, and that the only goal for an individual is unity with that force.

The Spread of Hinduism

During the Gupta period, which began in A.D. 320, the various cults of Hinduism also began to spread outside India and Sri Lanka. Rather than by missionaries or by military conquest, however, Hinduism spread through trade—the constant contact of Indian merchants and traders with the peoples of Southeast Asia. These traders often settled in foreign ports, bringing with them monks, priests, and books they had known in India.

The beliefs of India found a receptive audience in Southeast Asia. For example, local kings adopted the sacrifices of the Vedic religion in Borneo, and the cult of Shiva in what is now Vietnam. Legends from the *Ramayana* and the *Mahabharata* spread among the common people, and conforming laws governing dress, diet, behavior, and so on were passed. In what is now Indonesia, Hinduism arrived along with the *Ramayana* and the *Mahabharata*, and the people of Java adapted these epics to their own music, stories, dance, and the wayang, the Javanese theater of shadow puppets.

The Challenge of Islam

Eventually, the land of the Vedic religion and the bhakti cults was itself faced with invasion by a foreign religion—Islam. Beginning in the seventh century, Muslims, adherents of Islam, spread their faith by the sword, conquering and converting first the Middle East, northern Africa, and Persia (modern Iran), then the harsh desert frontiers of Pakistan and western India. By the eleventh century, Muslim conquerors had crossed these borders and were extending their rule to large parts of northern India.

But Islam had relatively little influence on Hindu beliefs. Some practices of the Muslims, such as the seclusion of wives and daughters, were adopted by Indians who remained practicing Hindus. But Islam itself was completely foreign to most Hindus. Muslims worshiped a single god, known by no earthly name, and recognized only a single holy prophet, Muhammad. They had no holy avatars such as Vishnu or Ganesha in their rituals or in their holy book, the Qur'an. Their religious ritual consisted of simple prayers that could be performed at any place. Muslims opposed the worship of graven images, such as statues or paintings: For a Muslim, God had no face or body that a human could describe, paint, or sculpt.

The Hindu gods and epics, however, influenced the faith of the newcomers. In some Muslim writings, Lord Krishna was adopted as an Islamic prophet. In addition, the Muslims brought with them a new cult known as Sufism, a sect that believed that all religions—Islam, Hinduism, Christianity—were different manifestations of the same divine revelations. According to Burton Stein: "Sufi teachers . . . were the purveyors of a mystic tradition which insisted on a personal bond between each believer and God, denying that either the institutions and offices of clerical interpreters or the laws of kings could replace it."[35]

Not only did Islam have little direct influence on Hindu beliefs, but relatively few Hindus chose to convert to Islam. Under Muslim rulers, the devotional bhakti cults and the works of art associated with them gained even wider acceptance among the ordinary people of India. As Kanitkar and Cole relate in *Hinduism:*

> Whether this flowering of devotional poetry would have occurred without the existence of Islam is again a debatable question. What can be said is that these and other bhaktas made God available to low caste and "outcaste" men and women, those outside caste on grounds of pollution, to the extent that conversion to Islam as the only way of gaining spiritual satisfaction was not necessary. Many low-caste people did convert, some for religious reasons; often,

however, the motive was social mobility; the hope of escaping from the rigidity of the caste system. Islam, however, failed to provide this relief, as did conversion to Christianity.[36]

The old habits of India could not be undone by a new religion brought into this vast country by outsiders. Instead, India and its faith absorbed Islam, which had to adapt itself to the new society and the new conditions it found.

Because it was so closely bound to everyday life, and with the arts and culture of India, and because it was a faith so individualized and personal to its believers, Hinduism proved strongly and successfully resistant to domination by foreign religions. In fact, Hinduism has spread in several different forms to many distant corners of the world, including Europe and North America. Certain forms of Hindu philosophy have intrigued Westerners for the last century, particularly the philosophy known as yoga.

Yoga and the West

Samkhya ("theory" or "knowledge") is the oldest school of Hindu philosophy, founded by the philosopher Kapila in the seventh century B.C. Its most important book, the *Samkhya-*

karika, was composed in about the third century A.D. Samkhya holds that there are two forces in the universe: souls or spirits *(purusha)* and nature or matter *(prakriti),* which exist bound up together. The goal of its teachings is the cessation of suffering—both physical and mental—which can be achieved by liberating the soul from the problems and worries of matter.

The individual who achieves this goal attains moksha—liberation from the cycle of reincarnation—and nirvana, an ultimate state of bliss.

To this end, the believer must study the ideas of Samkhya and practice the physical and mental exercises known collectively as yoga. According to the philosopher Patanjali, these exercises proceed in a series of eight stages:

Hindu worshipers at prayer. Other religions have had little influence on the Hindu faith.

1. Abstention (from violence, dishonesty, greed, theft, and sex);

2. Observance (of self-discipline and tolerance);

3. Posture (asana): the achievement of a steady and comfortable pose;

4. Control of breathing;

5. Withdrawal of the senses (such as what a person achieves during a deep sleep);

6. Concentrating the mind (emptying it of thoughts);

7. Meditation (often, on a single phrase or syllable);

8. Contemplation.

"Contemplation" in yoga means completely switching off the distracting thoughts that cloud and confuse the mind. In this final stage, a person senses the divine aspect of the physical world in the clearest manner possible. He or she has become independent from the world, a detached observer who has been freed from physical concerns entirely.

Joseph Campbell, in his book *Baksheesh and Brahman,* compares the process to stilling the waves on a pond:

If the wind dies down and the waters become perfectly still and clear, suddenly the whole perspective shifts and you are not seeing a lot of broken images, reflecting things about. You are looking down through the clear water to the lovely sandy bottom, and perhaps you will see fish in the water. The whole perspective changes and you behold, not a multitude of broken images, but a single, still, unmoving image.[37]

Yoga may be the aspect of Hinduism most familiar to people in the non-Hindu world. In fact, yoga schools and yoga exercises have been adopted by millions of people outside India who in no way consider themselves Hindus. In many cases, these yoga students are striving to achieve not only physical

Yoga masters like Richard Hittleman introduced yoga to America in the 1960s.

well-being through exercise, but also relief from the sometimes overwhelming stresses, worries, and rapid pace of modern life.

A System of Action

The Hindus of modern India know their religion as much more than the philosophies of yoga. They also know that the essence of Hinduism lies not in philosophy but in practice and ritual that takes place at certain times of day, certain seasons, and certain important stages of a person's life. Hinduism, as is often said by its practitioners, is a system of action, which holds the real key to the faith and to the beliefs of its followers.

chapter | four

The Practice of Hinduism

Each Hindu family holds its own tradition of belief and practice. Two neighboring families in an Indian town or village, who may be similar in every other way, may honor gods of different names and qualities. In the book *Voices from India,* a Hindu believer named Bhama Pandurang explains her own family's traditions:

> We are Vaishyas—the business caste. Our mother tongue is Telugu. We worship all the Hindu gods, but our family deity is Lord Venkateshwara, whose temple is at Triupati in Andhra Pradesh—the town of seven hills. He is a Vaishnavite god, but he is not worshipped only in the South. In the North he is known as Balaji.
>
> It is hard to explain just why a god is a family god to one family and not to another. It is a hereditary matter, and our family has worshipped Lord Venkateshwara for generations.[38]

The household gods, whoever they may be, provide only a single manifestation of Hindu belief. There are many others; but the man or woman who follows his or her dharma, and who follows a path meant to lead to enlightenment, is a Hindu. The many traditional rituals of Hinduism—daily, seasonal, and yearly rituals—mark this path.

The rituals of Hinduism have changed over time and vary from place to place. A family of Hindu immigrants in Britain has rituals of its own, passed down by the grandparents and parents, and which originated in a certain region or village of India. A family of rice farmers in southern India has rituals to express their devotion to the family's chosen deity, worship that might have originated thousands of years ago, long before the Aryans arrived in the north and the Rig-Veda was written down.

Early in the morning, a Hindu head of the household—either a husband or a wife—prepares for a daily family ritual known as the puja. The puja is performed before an image of the family's god, usually a statue of clay or stone but sometimes a painting. The characteristics and associations of the god are present—the elephant head of Ganesha, for example, or the blue face often given to Vishnu. The image is not considered an object of worship; its role is to fix the mind of the believer on the god.

One Hindu pandit, or scholar, explains the puja to an English traveler in this way:

To all these images we pay great honour; prostrating our bodies, and presenting to them, with much ceremony, flowers, rice, scented oil, saffron, and other similar articles. Yet we do not believe that these statues are themselves Brahma or Vishnu; but merely their images and representations. We show them deference only for the sake of the deity whom they represent, and when we pray it is not to the statue, but to that deity. Images are admitted in our temples, because we conceive that prayers are offered up with more devotion when there is something before the eyes that fixes the mind; but in fact we acknowledge that God alone is absolute, that He only is the omnipotent Lord.[39]

The statues, or murtis, are sometimes washed, then offered a gift of flowers and sometimes food. An incense stick is lit, along with a candle of ghee (clarified butter that does not smoke when it burns). The believer performs a namaskar, a gesture made by joining the hands and bowing. There follows a prayer or chant.

The puja of each individual may differ, but an individual's puja never varies from day to day. Bhama Pandurang describes her family's daily puja:

In the morning the heart is pure and uncontaminated by the worries of the day, so this is the time we offer our prayers. I prepare the puja room the night before for my husband. He is the master of the house and he does the most elaborate puja—it takes him nearly half an hour each day. He offers flowers, lights lamps of ghee, and recites the 108 names of Lord Venkateshwara. Lord Venkateshwara has a thousand names in all, but the full list is given only on festival days. Otherwise what businessman has time to spend three or four hours at puja—only elderly and retired persons can take so much time.[40]

The puja ritual might include the speaking of vratas (vows) for the protection and good fortune of a family. A Savitri Vrata is performed by a Hindu wife on behalf of a husband, while a Shashti Vrata is for one's children.

Public Rituals and Festivals

Religious observance by Hindus can be as private and personal as a puja ceremony or the speaking of vratas for

A Brahmin priest and his family perform the daily ritual known as puja.

the good fortune of the family. It can also be as public and exuberant as a crowded shrine procession, known as a rathayatra. The procession comes from a favorite practice of Indian royalty, when an entire city turned out to witness the parade of a local ruler with his family, his court followers, and his soldiers through the streets. The privilege of parading before the assembled people was extended to the images of the gods, who were taken from their temple homes once a year, or for important festivals, placed atop an elaborate ratha, or cart, and pulled or carried by crowds of people.

In addition to the public processions of the gods, Hindus observe many festivals to mark the changing seasons or to commemorate important events in Hindu mythology. Diwali, one of the best-known festivals throughout India and among Hindus living abroad, is a four-day celebration in October or November that originated in the ancient harvest ritual following a successful harvest. During Diwali, which means "arrangement of lamps," lamps are lit at dawn and late at night in every house, as families enjoy a feast and firecrackers are set off outside in the streets to celebrate the wealth and well-being of the community. On the second day of the festival, rice cakes are passed out, symbolizing the good harvest.

An Indian immigrant in America celebrates Diwali, the Hindu new year.

Traditionally, Diwali marked the start of the new year (which in ancient India occurred at the end of the fall harvest) and honored Lakshmi, the goddess of wealth, good luck, and beauty. Like all Hindu festivals, an elaborate mythology grew up around Diwali, as recounted by Sudheer Nirodkar:

According to mythology, the celebration of Diwali is closely bound up with one of India's two classic epics, the Ramayana. Lord Rama is said to have reigned for a long time during which the people were

The Lucky Sign: The Swastika

One Hindu emblem seen on temples, in artwork, and sometimes on people is a four-armed wheel known as the swastika, or "good fortune" sign. The swastika with its arms bent to the right reminds Hindu observers of the sun and the growth and evolution of the world. It represents the lengthening days and the seasons of spring and summer. The left-armed swastika, which turns counterclockwise, is a symbol of the declining sun and the shortening day, and thus represents autumn and winter.

As a symbol of protection, the swastika appears on the doors and lintels of Hindu temples and sometimes on the outside walls of private homes in India. To European eyes, however, the swastika represents anything but good fortune: Nazi Germany adopted the swastika as its symbol in the early twentieth century. Since then it has been seen in the West as a symbol of war, death, and the Holocaust, and is actually banned in modern Germany.

happy and contented. Ramrajya (the reign of Rama) has come to connote an era of peace and prosperity. The festival of Diwali . . . is celebrated to commemorate Rama's return from exile.[41]

Other festivals feature regional variations, although the underlying purpose does not change. Navaratri ("nine nights") is observed in a variety of ways all over India to celebrate fertility. It is dedicated to a goddess representing Mother Earth: Durga in some places, Kali in others. In western India, Hindu believers take part in marathon dances that circle a garbha, a lamp representing the womb, beginning in late evening and continuing through the night. In southern India, families dis-

play holy objects, artifacts, and toys. On the last day of the festival, effigies of certain figures—all representing enemies of Lord Rama—are burnt in public.

Some festivals, although celebrated by Hindus, are less religious in nature. Holi takes place in March and is the most public and least religious of all annual festivals: No god is honored and no rites are conducted inside the home. During this two-day event, the usual barriers between the sexes, the social classes, and among the different castes are forgotten. Celebrants light evening bonfires from scrap wood collected throughout the neighborhood. They run about, shouting, catcalling, joking, and tossing colored water and powder at each other. Holi is the

Hindu carnival, a time of revelry when the rules are eased and the people let loose. Writer Hema Nair, who as a child attended a private school run by Catholic nuns, describes the fun:

"Holi Mubarak! Happy Holi!" The morning air in Delhi rang with those words as my friends and I gleefully smeared blood-red or acid-green powder on our giggling victim. We poured blue or yellow powder on her hair, massaging it in for good measure. Balloons filled with water and gulal (pink powder) exploded with a wet thwack on her arms and legs as we shrieked for joy....

For a few hours that morning, all rules of etiquette drilled into us by the Irish nuns at school were cast aside, along with our prim pink-and-white uniforms. We were meant to be drenched with color that day, and our mothers made sure we left home wearing our oldest clothes. The naive victim who pleaded, "Stop, stop, please!" only invited more assaults.[42]

Hindus who emigrate often live with only memories of such public festivals, which are unknown in their new home countries. Many have created new holidays as alternatives to the holidays that their neighbors may celebrate. In the case of Christmas, for example, Hindus in the West have created an alternative known as the festival of Pancha Ganapati, a five-day observance that lasts from December 21 through December 25. This holiday honors Lord Ganesha, the elephant-headed god of wisdom and good luck. There are no wreaths, Santas, or trees, but celebrants exchange gifts and cards and hold feasts in their homes and, as recounted by writer Satguru Sivaya Subramuniyaswami:

Thousands of people take part in the Procession of the Elephants of Shiva.

Each day a tray of sweets, fruits, and incense is offered to Pancha Ganapati, often prepared and presented by the children. Chants, songs, and bhajanas are sung in His praise. After puja, sweets are shared as prasada. Each day gifts are given to the children, who place them before Pancha Ganapati to open only on the fifth day. Greeting cards are exchanged, always offering Hindu wisdom or verse from scripture.[43]

The Sva-Dharma

Each family of Hindu believers follows a particular code and way of life, known as its sva-dharma. The sva-dharma includes the particular festivals and rituals observed, the gods worshiped in the puja ritual, the observation of holy days, and customized beliefs about the gods and the world at large. It also involves the traditional *samskaras* (ceremonies) that a Hindu observes to mark the sixteen most important transitions in an individual's life. The first of these *samskaras* is the Namakarana festival, which takes place when a Hindu infant is not yet fully conscious of its family or of the wider world.

For ten days after birth, the Hindu mother and child are considered ritually impure, and no other member of the family has contact with them. On the twelfth day after birth, the family performs a naming ceremony. Friends and relatives are invited to the home, or to a public hall, where they observe the father and mother sitting side by side, with the baby on the mother's lap. The father writes the name of the baby alongside the date of its birth and the name of the family god, then whispers the child's name into his or her ear.

There are many traditions surrounding Hindu names. One says that male names should always consist of two or four syllables, while female names should have one, three, or five syllables. Non-Hindus often remark on the length and complexity of Hindu names; in the past, these names were composed of several different prefixes and suffixes, denoting the given name, the caste (varna), and traditional profession of the family (jati). Kanitkar and Cole explain: "In ancient days the male names were suffixed by specific words; Sharma for Brahmins, Varma for Kshatriyas, Gupta for Vaishyas and Dasa for Shudras. Thus the names might read Vishnusharma, Mahendravarma, Devagupta and Devadasa. Such names in modern Hindu society do not necessarily indicate varna or jati."[44]

Several more rituals are associated by Hindus with childhood. One rite marks the first time a baby eats solid food.

Another takes place the first time a boy (in some parts of India, also a girl) gets a haircut. The most important ritual of childhood for boys is the upanayana rite, also known as the sacred thread ceremony—an important preparation for the stages of life that follow.

The Sacred Thread

For a Hindu, life progresses in four stages, or asramas. The word *asrama* comes from *asram* (also ashram), a school where, according to Hindu tradition, students learned from knowledgeable gurus (teachers). These gurus advised the individual throughout his life on spiritual matters and on practical subjects such as homes, professions, and families. When giving instruction or advice, the guru took as his starting point the asramas and the student's proper progression through them.

During the first stage of life, brahmacarya, one gains wisdom, knowledge, and good judgment. Young Hindus are expected to gain physical and mental discipline with the guidance of parents and teachers. For boys, this stage of life begins with the study of the Hindu scriptures and texts, which is marked by the upanayana, also known as the sacred thread ceremony, which occurs between the ages of eight and eleven.

Hindus consider the sacred thread ceremony a kind of second birth; new studies will begin and new responsibilities are assumed. The elaborate preparation and ritual gives participants a sense of the importance of the occasion. Pandharinath Prabhu, in his book *Hindu Social Organization*, says this about the upanayana and other rites:

The samskaras and the elaborate ceremonies performed in association with them signify, both to the

A Hindu girl sits on a throne. It is a gift that marks her coming of age.

A young girl applies sacred powder to the forehead of a man to signal the beginning of the sacred thread ceremony.

individual as well as to the community, that something important is coming to happen to the individual on these particular occasions, in which both the community as well as the individual have their interests. Thus the Upanayana ceremony, for instance ... signifies that the individual is now to prepare himself to learn the community lore, for his own good as well as for that of the community.[45]

At the sacred thread ceremony, the young boy receives a sacred cord that he will wear under his clothing and around the left shoulder. The ritual marks the time when a youngster can begin hearing, reading, and understanding the most important mantras, prayers, and stories of the Hindu texts. He also learns the most important responsibilities of an adult, which are carried out in the second stage of life: garhasthya, the stage attained upon marriage to a suitable bride or husband.

Marriage and the Householder

The traditional wedding ceremony among Hindus is as elaborate as the family of the bride can afford and arrange. At one time, many wedding ceremonies and feasts continued for days, but the typical wedding in modern India is much shorter. After the guests take their place in the hall, the presiding priest gives an invocation of the family's gods as well as Ganesha, representing good fortune and future happiness. The bride arrives in her finest clothing, gold, and jewelry, and her mother greets the groom, who arrives later in the wedding hall. The couple exchange vows of duty and moderation and mutual support. They then tie the sacred thread around each other's wrists, symbolizing the marriage bond. They make offerings to a sacred fire, and then take seven steps to the north of the fire. Each step represents a mutual hope for the future: plentiful food, strength, wealth, happiness, children, mutual pleasures, and lifelong friendship.

The seven steps ceremony makes the marriage official. Afterward, the united bride and groom are given blessings by the assembled guests. The traditional wedding ends as the bride enters her new home, which is usually the household of her new husband. Kanitkar and Cole add:

The Occasional Ceremony

Some ceremonies are occasional—they are performed when an especially lucky event occurs, or when disaster strikes. In the late spring of 2001, the people of Nepal organized a rare exorcism ceremony known to Hindus as katto. *The occasion was a mass murder in the palace of the Nepalese king, who was gunned down with nearly his entire family, while gathered for dinner, by his own son, who also took his own life. The* katto *ceremony is a way of banishing evil influences and purifying an entire community. On the last day of official mourning for the king, a priest rode an elephant through the streets of Kathmandu, the Nepali capital, while crowds of people chased him to the edges of the city. As described in the ABC News online article "Hindu Ceremony Banishes Ghosts of Nepal Tragedy":*

"Durga Prasad Sapkota, 75, a senior Brahmin priest, rode the elephant . . . [in] a symbolic show of the spirit of the former king carrying the ills of the world into exile. He took with him a number of possessions belonging to the late king, including domestic items like a radio and television set."

In the evening the couple offer prayers to Ursa Major and the Pole Star. When the bride enters her new home, she is asked to kick a pot of grain at the threshold so that the grain will spill into the house, symbolically bringing prosperity into her new home. Then the bride is given a new first name symbolic of a new beginning.[46]

After marriage, a Hindu reaches the stage of grihasta settles into an occupation, and sets up a household. The householder raises a family and prepares the sons to carry on the family's name and traditions, including religious traditions. Sons leave the homes of their fathers to set up households of their own, while daughters join the households of their husbands.

The householder experiences the busiest, longest, and most important stage of life. He or she observes certain duties and obligations, including educating one's children, increasing the wealth and prosperity of the household, carrying out the proper rituals and pilgrimages, and seeing one's daughters properly married to suitable husbands. The householder who successfully carries out these obligations reflects well on the parents and teachers who trained him or her early in life.

Prosperity to a Hindu does not simply mean the size of one's house or the balance in one's bank account. According to the Bhagavad Gita, the ideal of the householder is selfless work carried out in the spirit of community. The fruits of labor are secondary; the good effects of a "right livelihood" are primary. Attaining these ideals brings freedom from self-regard and freedom from material wants, goals toward which all Hindus strive.

Final Stages

After the duties of a householder are carried out, the Hindu can look forward to vanaprasthya, or retirement and retreat from hard work and obligations. In this stage, a father turns over his household to his sons, who, he hopes, are well prepared to take the reins. According to tradition, the vanaprasthya stage begins when one's first grandson is born, an event that assures that the family's name will continue. The bonds that tie one to a single location and community gradually begin to loosen, and ordinary worldly goals are gradually left behind. At the stage of retirement, one can begin to return to the study and meditation of much higher goals that will be fulfilled at the end of one's life.

The sannyasa stage represents the final steps on this road. This stage brings complete renunciation of the ordinary world, and few take this path,

A sannyasi renounces the ordinary world in order to liberate himself from the chains of constant reincarnation.

as the sannyasi is a man who wanders the countryside like a hermit or lives in a monastery, without possessions, utterly dependent on the charity of others. The sannyasi takes vows of poverty and chastity; to symbolize this new existence he shaves his head and wears a bright ocher robe, or goes about completely naked. The sannyasi is seeking, through meditation and study, to achieve moksha, liberation from the chains of constant reincarnation.

If the head of a household chooses to become a sannyasi, family members know there is a good chance they will never see him again. For the sake of remembering, they may carry out an annual ritual. In some cases, the wives of men who become sannyasis are considered widows, and may marry again. Sannyasis may give up not only a normal life, but a normal death as well. The Hindu funeral ceremonies known as antyesti include a procession to a cremation site; the recitation of prayers, vows, and sacred texts; and an offering of flowers, food, drink, and other items for the dead for a period of ten days. But a sannyasi who dies without known male relatives is simply buried, and the cremation ceremony that is the duty of all Hindu sons is not carried out.

Hindus recognize several special classes of sannyasis. A dandi sannyasi carries an honorary staff or stick, which indicates that he is a teacher. To be recognized as a dandi, a Hindu must come from the caste of Brahmans. Brahmacaris, who must also belong to the Brahman caste, have abandoned the ordinary stages of life after their first stage of education. They are life-long sannyasis, who are celibate and who spend their entire adult lives as wandering ascetics.

A sannyasi known as a virakta gives up even speech and lives the simplest life possible, going about in a group of like-minded and silent sannyasis, reading the Hindu scriptures and practicing long stretches of meditation. The needs and desires of daily life are left completely behind, and long periods of fasting replace the ordinary routines of eating.

Although the virakta makes a frequent practice of fasting, going without food at least for brief periods is a practice common among Hindus of all kinds, at all stages of life. Going without food is always a voluntary act, never a requirement. A Hindu may fast on a certain day of the week or month, depending on the holiness of that day. For example, because Monday is sacred to the god Shiva,

some Shivaites might go without food between sunrise and sunset on this day. Doing so is believed to enhance the holiness of the day and bring a deity's blessing upon an individual or a household.

The Hindu Diet

The importance of fasting does not detract from the religious importance Hindus attach to eating and to diet. In general, the preparation of food and the manners of eating are very important to all Hindus.

Basically, Hindus recognize two different cooking methods: Food is either fried in ghee (pukka food) or cooked in water (katcha food). Pukka food can be preserved longer, and is believed not to pass on ritual impurity. Katcha food can pass on such so-called pollution in many ways: if it is handled by an impure person, such as a member of a lower caste; if it is exposed to impure water; or if an animal comes into contact with it by touching or smelling it. Food is also believed to be impure if it has been cooked twice, left overnight, or left from a previous meal.

Other Hindu dietary practices reflect the influence of other religions. The religious doctrine of ahimsa (non-violence), and the ban against harming certain animals, such as cows, originated among ancient religious ascetics, led by the prince Siddhartha Gautama, who founded Buddhism and who opposed the animal sacrifices practiced by the Vedic priests. Hinduism gradually incorporated this doctrine, and ahimsa is now practiced by many Hindus in the form of vegetarianism. Millions of Hindus, in Western countries as well as in India, eat no meat whatsoever. Furthermore, all Brahman priests go through life as vegetarians, and also will eat no onion or garlic, which are ritually polluting. The nineteenth-century French missionary J.A. Dubois wrote the following about Brahmans and food:

> There are as regard food three things which a Brahmin must avoid with the most scrupulous care: he must not eat anything that has had life or has even contained the principle of life; he must not drink intoxicating liquors; he must not touch food that has been prepared by persons of another caste. . . . I once met a Brahmin who, on seeing some eggs broken and beaten up for an omelette, immediately complained of feeling unwell, and in the course of a few moments was violently sick.[47]

Food not only represents an essential aspect of everyday living, but also carries religious significance. At its earliest

origins, the Vedic religion was a religion of sacrifice, and this notion survives in modern rituals such as the puja, in which the believer sacrifices a few grains of rice or a dish of ghee at the shrine of a household god. Food can also be brought to a shrine or temple outside the house, where it is offered in public to the god of a neighborhood or village. In such places, private worship

Sumptuous vegetarian dishes are served on banana leaves at a traditional Indian wedding feast.

and beliefs become public, and Hindus share communal observances.

Mandiras

For a Hindu, a sacred place of worship can be as small and close as a household shrine, or as vast and distant as one of the four holy rivers of India. The mandira (temple) of Hinduism can arise at an ordinary crossroads or in the center of an immense city. Hindus often state that there are as many temples in Hinduism as there are homes, as each dwelling where people observe rites at a shrine represents a home and shelter for a god.

Within the mandiras of India, the murti, or representation of the god to which the temple is dedicated, stands at the center. Worshipers arrive through a veranda, and reach the murti that stands in the garbhagriha ("womb-house"), the inner sanctum. Directly above the murti rises a spire, known as the shikhara. (In southern India, the spire is often replaced by a dome.) This structure denotes the sacredness of the building and of the sanctified murti within it.

The largest temples of India include several different buildings, each with unique functions. There may be a separate hall just to receive the offerings of pilgrims and worshipers. A dancing hall is open for the performances of temple dancers. A small stone slab that stands in front represents the vehicle used by the god, whether a bull, an eagle, or some other animal or bird. Smaller shrines may be situated around the main temple, each dedicated to the different names or forms of the principal god.

The consecration of the god is the act that officially sanctifies the Hindu temple. One of the Puranas, the instructive tales that were collected in written form beginning about two thousand years ago, lays down the procedure, which Kanitkar and Cole describe as follows:

> The statue is fully immersed in cold water. It is dried and the top of its head, eyes, ears, nose, mouth, chest, back, navel, arms and legs are touched with a piece of thin gold wire which is dipped in ghee and honey. It is then sprinkled with a mixture of milk, yogurt, ghee, sugar and honey, while mantras are recited. Afterwards it is bathed with cold water, dried, fixed on a pedestal in the inner shrine and offered an elaborate puja. After these rituals, the spirit of God is believed to enter the statute, which then becomes a murti to be worshipped as a symbol of the Divine Spirit.[48]

Distinctive towers mark Bali's Hindu temples.

One of the best-known temples of India is the Kalighat, a temple sacred to Kali that stands near the city of Calcutta, a sprawling urban center in northeastern India on the Bay of Bengal. The Kalighat was built in 1809 on the site of an older temple. According to one myth, when Sita, the wife of Shiva, died, her bereaved husband carried her body around the world, threatening to put an end to all creation. To avoid this unhappy result, Vishnu cut the body of Sita up into fifty-one separate pieces. The fragments fell to earth, lending sacred properties to each spot where they fell. The right toe fell on the site of Kalighat.

The Kalighat represents the destructive aspect of Kali. Each day a sacrifice is made here, and believers hold that the sacrifice satisfies the lust of blood and destruction of Kali. In this way, the Kalighat provides a link to the most ancient rites and sacrifices of the Vedic religion, the faith that eventually evolved into modern Hinduism.

chapter | five

Hinduism in the Modern World

Hindu believers use their faith to build a personal philosophy. Each believer develops an individual system of action and faith, each village honors its dominant gods and spirits, each sect has its leader and devoted followers. The basis of Hindu faith is right action, not correct belief. In an Internet discussion group, "A Discussion with Young American Hindus," teenager Arathi Subramanian explains her faith as follows:

> Duty and honor are the basis of the religion. I think all of the gods are only stories to portray these ideas. They are meant to teach us how we should live. How to be righteous and peaceful. That's the reason why we pray to God. We have the gods to show us what we are trying to be. For the main concepts of Hinduism you don't need all of the gods and all of the stories. To be called a Hindu you just need to be good.[49]

Gandhi's Modern Struggle

Exactly how to be good in a world that at times seems to reward or demand the opposite of goodness presents obvious difficulties. For many Hindus, this struggle was embodied in the person of the Indian statesman and spiritual leader Mohandas Gandhi, whom they nicknamed Mahatma, or "great soul."

Gandhi (1869–1948) gained a huge following among Hindus by practicing his personal dharma, by his own commitment to ahimsa (nonviolence), and by attaining a profound knowledge of himself and his limitations. The outward signs of his beliefs were wearing a simple dhoti, or loincloth, living quietly in a spare home, and spinning his own cotton yarn for the plain fabric of his clothes. Although he recognized and admitted his own imperfections, he followed the precepts of the Bhagavad Gita in renouncing passion as well as worldly ambition:

> To attain to perfect purity one has to become absolutely passion-free in thought, speech, and action; to rise above the opposing currents of love and hatred, attachment and repulsion. . . . That is why the world's praise fails to move me, indeed it very often stings me. To conquer the subtle passions seems to me to be far harder than the physical conquest of the world by

Hindus believe that Mohandas Gandhi (right) developed himself to the fullest by practicing his personal dharma.

A Subcontinent Divided

Gandhi's protest against British laws and domination of India had the effect of rallying a vast subcontinent of diverse castes, beliefs, languages, and rituals to a common cause, that of Indian independence. But the achievement of independence was tainted by the ongoing conflict between Hindus and Muslims in India. Gandhi believed Hindus and Muslims could live together peacefully, and he saw the partition of India and Pakistan as a disaster. In January 1948, just after breaking a fast to protest fighting between Hindu and Muslim believers, he was assassinated by a Brahman Hindu who was angered by Gandhi's doctrine of religious tolerance.

the force of arms....I must reduce myself to zero. So long as a man does not of his own free will put himself last among his fellow creatures, there is no salvation for him.[50]

Caste in Modern India

Gandhi is best known in his role as an advocate of Indian independence, but he also struggled against long-held traditional beliefs and cultural institutions among his fellow Hindus. One of these institutions—the system of caste—came to symbolize the difficulty of India's transformation from ancient society to modern democracy. It is one of the most intractable of all problems, because caste still forms a basis for what Hindus do, how they act toward others, and how they see themselves in society.

Much of what Westerners know, or think they know, about caste arises from misunderstandings, which began

when the first Portuguese explorers arrived in India and gave one of their own words *(casta)* to the social system they observed among the natives.

Many historians believe that caste originally began with the Aryans, who considered the non-Aryan peoples they conquered an inferior social class. The brahmans, or priests in charge of sacrificial offerings, occupied a very high rung on the social ladder, and eventually this group evolved into the highest and most religiously pure caste, or class, within India, membership in which is inherited and with which millions of modern Indians identify themselves. As historian Burton Stein explains:

Aryans of the early Rigveda were organized into tribes (jana), and further divided into ruling lineages (rajanya), and commoner clans (vis). By degrees, some of the ruling clansmen took another title, "kshatriya," from the word *kshatra*, or power, and they along with the most adept of the priestly ritualists (brahmans) constituted the elite of society, each group contributing to the welfare and interests of the other.[51]

In Hindu society, such social divisions exist to this day, most broadly in the form of four main classes known as varnas:

1. Brahmans, originally members of the priestly caste, and now the caste of priests as well as religious teachers. Members of the Brahman caste are considered the most knowledgeable and enlightened of society, and are held to strict practices to maintain ritual purity;

2. Kshatriyas, the varna of soldiers, aristocrats, and administrators. Traditionally, the kshatriyas were leaders who, through their skill and experience, governed and protected the rest of society;

3. Vaishyas, or merchants and farmers, who carried on such trades as shopkeeping, trading, banking, and all kinds of agriculture;

4. Sudras, or servants, who rendered their labor and service to members of the other varnas.

The caste system does not end with the four main varnas. There are hundreds of smaller divisions, known as jati, with which Hindu families are identified and which signify the practice of particular occupations. Within the Sudra varna, for example, are specific jatis for barbers, ditchdiggers, and so on.

Traditionally, particular professions were assigned to certain jatis and handed down from father to son to grandson. Many rules connected with caste determined social position and behavior. Members of the upper castes, for example, would not eat food prepared by members of lower castes, as they considered the food impure, and would not share water from the same well. Certain Hindu temples were consecrated to the members of certain varnas, and members of the lower orders were not permitted to enter or worship in them. Sons and daughters were expected to marry within the caste, a rule that was intended to keep traditional religious beliefs and practices in the family.

A Hindu is born into his or her jati and cannot leave it, regardless of his actions or his beliefs. It has not always been this way, however, as Kanitkar and Cole explain:

> In the early period . . . it was possible for some people to change

their occupations, and to move either up or down the first three varnas. . . . As time went on, various occupations became exclusive, and each group created a vested interest in its own particular occupation, thus making it very difficult for people to change their jobs. Occupations became hereditary and exclusive to certain groups, giving rise to rules prohibiting intermarriage and dining between castes.[52]

In modern India, especially in cities, and among Hindu communities outside India, the caste system has undergone important changes. Although all Hindus still recognize their family's membership in a specific jati, caste is no longer a barrier to entering certain professions. For example, a business in India will not require applicants for jobs to belong to a certain caste—although loyalty to a caste may persuade an employer to hire a certain applicant. Nor do universities require all students to come from the same caste. Members of the lowest varna, the Sudras, can reach the highest levels of the Indian government and win election to the legislature.

Many Hindu teachers and philosophers have set themselves firmly against any religious basis for the caste system. One of these is Swami

Vivekenanda, one of the world's best-known teachers of Hinduism. Vivekenanda treats caste as follows in his book *Swami Vivekenanda on India and Her Problems:*

> Though our castes and our institutions are apparently linked with our religion, they are not so. These institutions have been necessary to protect us as a nation, and when this necessity for self-preservation will no more exist, they will die a

Young Brahmins stand in neck-deep water praying to the Hindu god of rain.

natural death. In religion there is no caste. A man from the highest caste and a man from the lowest may become a monk in India and the two castes become equal. . . . Caste is simply a crystallized social institution, which after doing its service is now filling the atmosphere of India with its stench, and it can only be removed by giving back to people their lost social individuality.[53]

The Untouchables

All social institutions define members and outsiders, and the caste system is no different. Hindus recognize that certain professions lie outside the caste system altogether. These occupations, such as handling dead bodies or tanning leather, are considered ritually unclean. Those who hold this position in society are without caste, and also known as "untouchable." Traditionally, they were believed to have the effect of polluting everything they touched, and contact with them caused impurity that had to be amended through a ritual of purification. They were barred from holding most jobs, prohibited from entering Hindu temples, and generally shunned by the rest of society. In modern India, the untouchables are also known as dalit.

Historians debate the origin of the untouchables, or "outcastes." Mark

An Indian cobbler, a member of the dalit class, repairs shoes at his stand.

Sullivan suggests these possibilities: "Some groups may have been classified as Outcaste because they were tribal groups not assimilated by Brahmanical culture; others may once have been in the caste system but lost their status because of failure to perform appropriate rituals or to observe social strictures."[54]

During the twentieth century, the marginalization of the dalit came under increasing censure in a modernizing Indian society. The outcaste status of the untouchables was legally abolished in India in 1950. The dalit can now hold any kind of job for which they may be qualified by experience or training. Universities and government offices hold open a percentage of their placements to the dalit in a kind of Hindu affirmative action. By law, the dalit cannot be barred from entry to Indian universities. In many ways, the untouchables have made great progress beyond their old status and stand equal to Indians of any caste.

Yet millions of Hindus still see themselves as members of the dalit society and thus "outside" the caste system. This has led to violent confrontations within India, where "outcastes" (and those of low caste) still see themselves on the lowest rungs of the social ladder, prevented by old traditions from improving their lot in life. This status is also still recognized as an significant barrier in one of the most important institutions of any society: marriage.

During a marriage ceremony, the couple circles a fire seven times to formalize their union.

Marriage

Among Hindu families, as in the rest of the world, the marriage of sons and daughters is a vitally important as well as worrisome event. One of the primary duties of a Hindu mother or father is to ensure that the traditions of the family are carried on in the generations to follow. Most Hindu families also still seek to have sons and daughters married within their own caste. As a result, the tradition of arranged mar-

riage, which has disappeared in the West, has survived in India.

Many Indians believe that arranged marriages help preserve the family traditions, business, beliefs, and ritual practice. But to find a suitable marriage partner from an appropriate family is not always easy. Many parents carry out a search in the classified sections of modern Indian newspapers. One such marriage ad for a prospective husband, given in *Voices from India,* goes as follows: "Alliance invited from parents of Smartha Brahmin officers, engineers, doctors, professors, business executives or similar status for … post-graduate girl, 23, 5'4", slim, medium complexion, expert in Carnatic vocal, modern arts, crafts, household duties and car driving."[55]

Arranged marriages used to be the norm in India, and remain the standard practice in many families. Although some young women marry for love, many others marry with the guidance of parents. They undergo a very close inspection by their future in-laws, and in the meantime have very little contact with their prospective husbands before the wedding ceremony. Although most women have the right to refuse to marry a husband selected for them, they are still expected to win the approval of their parents—which will come on the basis of background and caste—before marrying anybody.

Central to the complex negotiations and arrangements of marriages is the dowry, a payment of money or gifts brought by the woman to the husband's family. The dowry, like many other traditional institutions, is undergoing change. By a law passed in 1961, dowries were officially banned in India, but the custom survives in the form of wedding presents, which, like betrothal, can be the subject of elaborate negotiation.

The West Arrives

Just as marriage institutions are being challenged, the workaday world of the

Bali's Hinduism

In the early twenty-first century, the island of Bali remains a Hindu stronghold within largely Islamic Indonesia. The Balinese set themselves apart as a distinct ethnic group marked most importantly by religion. They adopted the forms, but not the customs, of the Indian caste system, as described in Indonesia, *a Library of Congress study by William H. Frederick and Robert L. Worden.*

"Like the Javanese, Balinese society is stratified. It possesses the small hereditary Brahmin class, as well as small groups of Vaishya and Kshatriya classes that draw on Indian caste terminology. However, the Balinese caste system involves no occupational specializations or ideas about ritual contaminations between the ranks. It does not prohibit marriage between ranks, but does forbid women to marry beneath their class."

married householder has also changed, as modern India is increasingly exposed to commerical, entertainment, and cultural influences from the outside world. Two centuries of British colonization made English a principal language of government and media within India. Hindus who emigrate from India to the English-speaking nations thus are easily familiarized with new customs, which in turn are imported to India by global media, by business contacts, and by emigrants returning home to visit their families and hometowns.

This "invasion" of Hindu India by Western culture poses problems, as a religious authority named Sri Jayendra Saraswait explains:

> Western culture is riddled with contradictions between words and deeds while the eastern is all about harmony between words and action.... It is with the ushering in by the West, or an industrial culture in the country [India], there has come into existence a culture of "work by the wristwatch." With the Western orientation, a hedonistic, pleasure-seeking culture too has crept in.[56]

In other words, Western-style work and prosperity bring a new set of problems that directly affect the foundations of Hinduism. Not only do foreign nations influence Indian society, but the lures of a prosperous West prove irresistible to young Indians, who immigrate to Europe, the United Kingdom, and the United States. As a result of this migration, India loses talented and energetic young people who represent a valuable resource for India's future (although declining population has never been a pressing problem in India, where the population has reached more than 1 billion).

Within India, popular culture also poses a challenge to Hindu traditions. Movie stars and pop singers draw more attention among the young than do the hoary deities of millennia-old epics. The ordinary rebelliousness of the young is intensified by the attractions of a secular lifestyle. Instead of adopting the gods and faith of his or her parents, the young Hindu of the twenty-first century may throw off the religion altogether. Like his or her contemporary in Europe or the United States, religion may be forgotten, or become just a part of the study of history and literature and not the basis for right action or right living.

Yet Hinduism has left a permanent mark on Indian psyche, and Indians find many aspects of life in the West strange indeed. In his book *India:*

The Bandit Queen

One of the most famous, and most violent, "outcaste" outlaws was Phoolan Devi, a modern woman born into a family of boatmen. Devi was married by arrangement at the age of eleven and, according to her version of her life, was constantly beaten by her husband. Nevertheless, she grew into a capable and intelligent woman, and once defended her father in court over a land dispute. But she was soon afterward arrested, imprisoned, and assaulted by policemen. She escaped, joined a gang of outlaws, then was captured and raped again.

When Phoolan Devi returned to the wilderness, she set out on a mission of revenge. She gathered several followers, armed her group, and assassinated more than twenty of the men she believed had mistreated her. In 1983 she turned herself in to the authorities and was imprisoned, but not before becoming a symbol of the need for greater rights and better treatment for women and low-caste Indians. After her release in 1994, she ran for and won a seat in India's parliament.

Phoolan Devi earned the nickname of "the Bandit Queen." A movie by the same name was made of her life. She had gained a national following; many Hindus admired her and believed her to be an incarnation of Kali, the goddess of fear, bloodshed, and destruction. But she had also made many enemies during her career. The families of the murdered men vowed their own revenge against her, and it may have been one such enemy that carried out her assassination on July 24, 2001.

Phoolan Devi has become a symbol of the poor treatment of women from India's low castes.

Labyrinths in the Lotus Land, Sasthi Brata described this confrontation and mutual misunderstanding between Indian and Westerner:

> Indians don't look at life in ... black-and-white, either/or terms. The predominant religion, Hinduism, accepts passivity as a virtue; the Bhagavad Gita specifically instructs its adherents not to seek the rewards of their own endeavors—a far cry from the Protestant work ethic in the majority of the Western world.[57]

Brata goes on to note that Hindus do not necessarily envy Westerners, however:

> If the Westerner finds the Indian occasionally fascinating, but more often pathetic, he may be surprised to discover that the object of his condescension feels enormous sympathy for his Occidental [Western] afflictions—too much reliance on material comforts, an obsession with time, a total neglect of the "meditational" aspects of life.[58]

Hinduism can also be contrasted sharply with Western culture in its treatment of the final transformation of life, physical death. Hindus attend to the death of the individual with as much ceremony and ritual as they attend to birth, the passage into adulthood, and marriage. But like these other life stages, the beliefs surrounding death are subtly changing in modern India.

Death in Modern India

For Hindus, death marks not the end of life but only transformation from one incarnation to another. For most believers, cremation is the preferred form of carrying out this transition. One of the most astounding sights in modern India is the row of funeral pyres that line the banks of the sacred Ganges River, throwing flames into the sky and black smoke along the riverbank. The river is considered sacred but pure—many Hindus bring a small vial of Ganges River water with them on their travels away from home. It remains the devout wish of many Hindus to have their ashes mingled with the waters of the Ganges.

Among at least some Hindus, however, concern is growing not for the life to come but for the life they and other Hindus are leaving behind. The modern age and the environmental movement have brought new outlooks and new concerns regarding the disposal of their remains. Raghubir Singh, in his book *The Ganges,* explains:

> I must confess . . . that before the late 1970s pollution in the Ganga

Cremation on a funeral pyre aids transformation from one incarnation to another.

did not bother me. I did what almost all Indians did, I ignored it. This attitude has now changed dramatically. The Western environmental movement has taken root in India.

But the task of cleaning the Ganga is entirely uphill. At Banaras alone 40,000 bodies are cremated every year. Although electric crematoria have slowly taken hold along the entire river, many bodies are still tossed into the Ganga half-burnt. Dead animals are thrown in without a thought to pollution. Holy men and women, those who die from disease, and rajas are not cremated. After appropriate cere-monies their bodies are tied to large stones and cast into the Ganga.[59]

The pollution of the sacred Ganges River is one of many social and environmental problems that modern India faces. In many ways, the beliefs of Hinduism are being transformed in the modern world in which "globalization" is demanding more uniform economic and social practices. Although some see this process as a threat to Hinduism (and to other world religions), many of its adherents see Hinduism as the faith best adapted to changing conditions and as the last best hope for the nations of the world to avoid future violence, warfare, and destruction.

chapter | six

Modern Challenges to Hinduism

As the twenty-first century begins, Hindus face many of the same problems that believers in other world religions face. Modern technologies, such as computers and satellite television, include little room for religious thought or contemplation. The drive to succeed in a competitive global economy—a drive that is bringing drastic changes to India—makes heavy demands on available time, competing with religious observances, ceremonies, and festivals. New technologies, in the view of many, are also leading to secularization of society to such an extent that religious doctrines have no importance whatsoever.

India is dealing with a new kind of invasion—a wave of foreign culture that arrives via computer, television, and film. Western culture is especially difficult to resist because it brings uniformity. People sharing instant worldwide communication and international media expose themselves to similar influences. As a result, their lifestyles, their habits, and their patterns of thought and opinion tend to merge. This directly contradicts one of the most important tenets of Hinduism: its acceptance of diversity. In the past, Hinduism tolerated the worship of many different gods, many different philosophies, and many differents ways of worship. Each family had a tradition of its own: a certain household god, a certain chant for the morning puja. Some people devoted themselves to Vishnu, others to Shiva. Thousands of local gods and ceremonies made the Indian subcontinent a complex religious mosaic of wildly contrasting parts.

The effects of the modern age may change what had been a mosaic of religious practice into a more uniform faith in which variety lessens and dharma becomes similar from one family and believer to the next.

Hindus and Muslims

The trend toward more uniformity within Hinduism also threatens to change how Hindus relate to individuals of other faiths. For the most part, Hindus still accept a wide variety of beliefs and rituals. Hindus in India, however, coexist with Muslim believers in several regions of the country, and religious differences have brought about a sharply divided society, especially in the north. Since India's independence from Britain (and occasionally before), there have been violent riots between Muslims and Hindus in many Indian cities. Hindu-Muslim antagonism has inspired assassinations, bombings, arson, and a pervasive feeling of mutual mistrust.

Bruce Sullivan, in *Historical Dictionary of Hinduism*, describes the problem:

The definition of "Hinduism" is politically and socially significant in India today. As a democracy, India is governed by majority rule. India's census reports that about eighty-three per cent of its citizens are "Hindu" while eleven per cent are Muslim, the remaining six per cent including Sikhs, Christians, Jains, Buddhists, and a few others. Some Hindu nationalists insist that all who are not Muslim or Christian are Hindu, taking "Hindu" more in a cultural than a religious sense. Some even go so far as to suggest that those who are not in the Hindu category, as they define it, should not be citizens of India.[60]

The hostility between Hindus and Muslims goes back centuries. Muslim rule in India began with a sultanate that was established in Delhi in the early thirteenth century. Then, in 1526, came an invasion of India by Babar, a Muslim conqueror from the central Asian kingdom of Samarkand. Babar's establishment of the Mogul Empire was accompanied by frequent clashes between Muslim rulers and their Hindu subjects in northern India. In the eighteenth century, the gradual British conquest of India ended Muslim rule. The British were Christians, but their goal in India was

A building burns during an outbreak of hostility between Hindus and Muslims.

trade and profit, not conversion, so they tended to leave India's Hindus and Muslims to continue their respective religious practices.

After India won its independence in 1947, the question of whether India should be ruled by its Hindu majority became an urgent concern. Over the objections of many of India's leaders, the new nation was partitioned. Pakistan was founded as a Muslim nation, and Western leaders, at least, believed that providing Muslims with a nation of their own would solve the problem of Hindu-Muslim conflict. But the founding of Pakistan failed to end centuries of mistrust.

The conflict between Hindu India and Muslim Pakistan has periodically erupted in outright war. In 1965 and again in 1971, the two nations fought over which nation should control the disputed territory lying between them, including Kashmir and the Punjab. Although these ongoing conflicts have been over territory and natural resources, always just below the surface and exacerbating mutual suspicion have been matters of faith.

The threat of fighting still looms over India's long frontier with Pakistan. Making any dispute far more dangerous is the fact that both countries now possess nuclear weapons. Hindus boast that they have never invaded anyone, that the Hindu religion has never been forced on a non-Hindu people at the point of a sword. Yet India has shown itself more than willing to confront its neighbor on many occasions.

Within India, violence between Hindus and the Muslim minority occurs regularly. The two factions air their antagonism in their political parties, in newspapers and other media, and in large and small commercial interests. At the village level, Muslims and Hindus compete for water, land, and other resources. Neighborhoods in large cities are marked out as belonging to one religion or the other, and become hostile territory to those of different faiths.

Revivalism

As the twenty-first century opens, a Hindu revival movement makes up an important ingredient in this volatile mix. There have been many revival movements in the past in which inspired and charismatic leaders attempt to return the faith to its roots

Apu: All-American Hindu

The United States is far from India, and many Americans know Hindus and their faith only through images on television and film. One of the most familiar characterizations of Hindus to many people in the United States is animated: Apu Nahaasapeemapetilon, a convenience-store clerk in the satirical television series The Simpsons. *As described by writer Mark I. Pinsky in his Internet article "Apu: Springfield's Intro to Hinduism":*

"In many ways, the character is stereotypical of Asian immigrants to North America, and a model minority member. Born in Pakistan, Apu and his family migrated to Ramatpur in India, and later studied at the Calcutta Institute of Technology ("CalTech"), where he graduated at the top of his class of seven million. . . .

However, not all of the stereotypes Apu embodies are positive. For example, he is apparently a Hindu nationalist: on the shelf in his apartment is a record album entitled 'The Concert Against Bangladesh,' with a mushroom cloud on the cover, obliterating India's poverty-stricken Muslim neighbor. . . . Yet next to Marge, Apu is probably the most good-hearted and saintly character on "The Simpsons," qualities presented on the show as an outgrowth of his Hindu faith and of his Indian culture. At his dinner table, with Homer and Marge as guests, he recites a grace that is clearly a parody of one familiar to the Simpsons: 'Good rice, good curry, good Gandhi, let's hurry.'"

and, at the same time, make it meaningful and relevant to a changing world. For example, in the early nineteenth century, the Brahmo Samaj movement, led by Ram Mohan Roy, condemned many of the ancient rituals and old customs such as child marriage and the caste system. Later in the century, while India was still under British control, Swami Dayanand Sarasvati founded the Arya Samaj movement. He preached the practice of Hinduism strictly according to the teaching of the Vedas, without the various aspects later added to them, particularly the worship of images. Sarasvati also taught that caste membership should be based on merit, and not on heredity.

Hindu revivalism took on a more overtly political tone following Indian independence. After the partition of India and Pakistan, Hindu revivalists continued to fight for a pure Hindu nation, free of the influence of religions they considered foreign to the Indian nation, particularly Islam. These sentiments brought about the founding of the Bharatiya Janata Party (BJP) in 1980. The BJP fights for the return of Hinduism as the dominant institution in the civic life of India.

For many who fought for Hindu revival, more than just Islam was seen as a threat. The 1980s saw not only the growth of the BJP movement but also out-and-out war between the government of India, led by Indira Gandhi, and the Sikhs of the Punjab region. Under the rule of the Akali Dal, the main Sikh political party, Punjab had become an increasingly autonomous state within India. The Punjab had become one of the most prosperous regions of India, and the hardworking Sikhs made up a substantial percentage of professionals, government leaders, and military officers in the rest of India. To the present day, the Indian government and Punjabi Sikhs struggle for control of the region.

Hindu-Muslim Conflict

Modern Hindu nationalism came to a climax in 1992 when a crowd of Hindu believers stormed the Babri Masjid mosque in the northern Indian city of Ayodhya. Hindu political leaders claimed that the mosque was located on a spot sacred to Hindus—the birthplace of the god Ram—and that a Hindu shrine had been destroyed centuries ago on the same place.

The storming of the Babri Masjid mosque touched off riots and violence that flared up periodically for years, and it remains a very sore point between Hindus and Muslims. For many Hindus, Islam still represents

The Indian government and the revivalist Sikhs (pictured) continue to fight over the Punjab region.

an invasion and rule of their country by foreigners. Muslims, for their part, still resent their status as outsiders, even though have been living in India for centuries, as the essayist Ankur Shah reveals:

Muslims have an acute sense of insecurity. . . . [They] complain of educational and economic backwardness. Although Muslims comprise over twelve percent of the population, their school population is less than two percent. Muslims are lagging behind Hindus in professional areas as well, and are under-represented in government employment, armed services, and police forces.[61]

Muslims also feel that the government of India will do nothing to help them. They point to the founding of the BJP, which very briefly took control of the Indian government in 1996. They watch closely the rivalry of India and Pakistan over Kashmir, a predominantly Muslim northern province of India that is claimed by both countries. They also note the symbolism of decisions such as the renaming of the city of Bombay to Mumbai, after the name of a Hindu goddess.

Working-class and poor Hindus, however, have their own long list of grievances, and see their only hope in the militancy of the BJP and a routing of Muslims from their midst. Hinduism, for these people, represents a political action program and not just a religious faith. Shashi Tharoor, in *India: From Midnight to Millennium*, describes the bewildering changes that have thrown India into its modern turmoil:

> The youths who smashed the Babri Masjid wore the shirts and trousers of lower-middle-class urban youth, men whose opportunities have not matched their expectations, and who are taking out their resentment on the visible Other. Various sections of Hindu society are seeing their status and privileges threatened by bewildering processes of change: affirmative-action programs for Dalits [outside-caste or "untouchables"] and "backward classes," trade liberalization, economic reforms that have brought foreign employers, remittances [money sent home] from [Persian] Gulf labor that have made nouveaux riches out of their Muslim neighbors. A

worldview resting on the timeless assumptions has been jolted by the realization that you can't take anything for granted anymore.[62]

Secularization

If relations with those of other faiths serve as one focus of the BJP's attention, another is the secular influence of multinational corporations. The BJP and Hindus sympathetic to it also oppose foreign intrusions into India's economic life. In the 1990s, these protests were often focused on Western fast-food chains such as McDonald's and Kentucky Fried Chicken, which opened franchises in Indian cities. The protest against KFC is documented by Tharoor:

> The KFC store in Bangalore . . . was trashed by a farmers' mob, which burst in after well-publicized protests and ransacked the premises. Subtler techniques were used in Delhi, where, in response to a legal complaint, the outlet was closed by a magistrate because two flies were found buzzing around the kitchen. . . .
>
> The hostility to KFC is less . . . about real economic damage to Indians than it is about politics. The enemies of Kentucky Fried Chicken are decrying not their sales but the

sellout, by the Indian government, to Western influences.[63]

The Fashion of Hinduism

Many Hindus who move to European nations or to the United States are faced with the difficulty of practicing their religion amid the very different culture that surrounds them, influencing their lifestyle and their children's behavior and opinions. Hindus in Britain, the United States, and elsewhere have built their own temples; they hold services and carry out, in their own family traditions, the rites of birth, marriage, and death. But Hindu practices can increase their sense of estrangement from the much larger Christian community that is often hostile toward them. Like people everywhere, they want to adapt to the society they live in, with the result that their ancient faith and its expression fades into the background. Their children, born in a place where Hinduism is seen as strange and foreign, seek to join peers who may feel little interest in religion

The Golden Temple

Prime minister Indira Gandhi refused to accept the independence of the Sikh-dominated Punjab, which by 1983 had found its rallying place at the Golden Temple, a magnificent sixteenth-century edifice in the city of Amritsar. The religion of the Sikhs, which had begun as a renewal and revival of traditional Hinduism, had become a focal point of opposition to the rest of India.

The most holy building of all the Sikhs, the Golden Temple rose from a large reflecting lake, and shone with walls and towers made of gold leaf. From this place, the Sikh leader Bhindranwale directed a campaign of terror against the Indian government with bombings and assassinations, which made the Punjab a very dangeorus place for anyone who opposed him. Finally, in May 1984, a violent confrontation took place at the Golden Temple. The Sikhs who had barricaded themselves within the temple fought against tanks and heavy artillery of the regular Indian army.

More than one thousand people died, and thousands were injured. The Golden Temple was destroyed. Enraged and humiliated, the Sikhs vowed revenge, which they took on October 31 of the same year, when Indira Gandhi was shot down by two of her own Sikh bodyguards.

in general or in Hinduism in particular. Their Hindu beliefs and rituals begin to fall out of fashion.

The writer Shoba Narayan, in her Internet article "Indian or Hindu: One, Both, or Neither?" describes a common situation:

> My sister-in-law in Florida, for example, is a devout Hindu, who prays before her altar every morning before going off to the hospital to treat patients. But her kids identify more with being of Indian descent than being Hindus. For them, putting up a Christmas tree is equally important as celebrating Diwali, if not more so. In fact, I would guess that Hinduism is a marginal part of their identity. . . . They have Hindu names: Balaji, Ravi, Nitya, Sita; many of them are vegetarians; they know Hindu bhajans even though they rarely sing them; and they even know a Sanskrit sloka (chant) or two. But these Hindu values take the back seat to their being Indian.[64]

In the modern world, both inside and outside India, religion has become disconnected from everyday life. Faith and ritual play minimal roles in the working world, and religious practice is limited to a special place in the home or a special day of the week. The general opinion of Hinduism among Hindus also changes over time, going in and out of fashion. In an editorial entitled "Why Do Hindus Say, 'I Am Not a Hindu'?", one editor explains:

> From century to century, overt affiliation with Hinduism becomes faddish and then fusty in cycles. In recent years it has become voguish for Hindus to openly and proudly proclaim themselves. Five decades back, being a Hindu was not cool, what with the Anglican British in charge and all. Nine decades back, Swami Vivekenanda, bucking the anti-Hindu fashion of the late 1800s, spoke proudly of his Hinduism, and called on others to do the same, as did Gandhi, Sri Aurobindo, and Swami Dayananda. And so it goes, see-sawing back and forth.[65]

As Seen in the West

Hinduism also goes through similar cycles in the Western world. In the past, it was viewed in the West as a pagan religion, mainly because of its many gods. In the nineteenth century, however, Western travelers took up the study of Hinduism. Hindu philosophers, moreover, made the journey to Great Britain and the United States. Hindu beliefs in death and reincarnation held great interest

Hinduism and the Movies

The famously prodigious film industry in India is more than an entertainment medium. At the movies, Indians often see in the plots and characters a contest of ideas, a fictionalized debate of important national, political, and social issues. Indian directors have fierce partisans and detractors, and a few idolized Indian screen actors have become semidivine figures.

A national censoring board carefully reviews each film and has the power to order changes in those likely to cause trouble. Nevertheless, films that address controversial subjects quickly become controversial themselves. In 1992 the director Mani Rathnam produced Bombay, *a film set among riots between Hindus and Muslims. In an essay published on the Internet site "India in New York," www.indiainnewyork.com, writer Subhash K. Jha describes the consequences:*

"Mani Rathnam's 'Bombay,' based on the communal riots in the city in 1992, had portrayed the horror and trauma of a young Hindu man and his Muslim wife during the riots. The film angered Muslim groups across the country. Some groups even threatened owners of cinema theaters screening 'Bombay' with dire consequences. A bomb was hurled at Rathnam's residence in Chennai.

After 'Bombay,' most filmmakers decided to avoid the sensitive issue of intercommunal romances and marriages. But in 1998, in 'Zakhm,' director Mahesh Bhatt took up the theme once again, portraying the true-life relationship between his Muslim mother and his Hindu father. The censor board ordered that Bhatt delete some scenes it said were communally sensitive before the film was released commercially."

for Victorian society, in which spiritualism provided Christian believers with an outlet for natural human curiosity in the afterlife. Spiritualism based on Hindu philosophy found two important proponents in Henry Steele Olcott and Helena P. Blavatsky, who cofounded the Theosophical Society in the United States in the 1870s. Ironically, theosophy influenced Hindus in India as well.

Blavatsky and Olcott traveled to India and taught many English-speaking Hindus greater respect for their traditional beliefs at a time when British colonialism was dominating the Indian economy as well as culture and Hinduism was in decline as a result.

The English Theosophical leader Annie Besant struck the following note for preservation of traditional Hinduism within India:

After a study of some forty years and more of the great religions of the world, I find none so perfect, none so scientific, none so philosophic and none so spiritual as the great religion known by the name of Hinduism. . . . Make no mistake, without Hinduism, India has no future. Hinduism is the soil into which India's roots are struck, and torn out of that, she will inevitably wither, as a tree torn out from its place.[66]

Hinduism continues to challenge other faiths in the West. In the twentieth century, many Westerners looked on Hinduism as an "alternative" religion, a faith taken up by the young and the curious, or those seeking relief from modern stress and conflict. But in the minds of many in the West, Hinduism was also associated with cults—groups that isolate themselves from society, are led by charismatic leaders, and indoctrinate their members, sometimes by threat or force, in their particular beliefs and way of life.

One such cult, as it was seen by many Westerners, is the Hare Krishna movement, founded by Swami A.C. Bhaktivedanta Prabhupada. This teacher founded the International Society for Krishna Consciousness (ISKCON), moved to the United States, and founded schools in several American cities. Some (not all) Hare Krishna members left their ordinary lives behind, lived in communal groups, and adopted the orange clothing of the Indian sannyasi. Members spent much of their time in public places, such as parks and airports, distributing literature and soliciting new members, and chanting a simple mantra:

Hare Krishna, Hare Krishna, Krishna, Krishna, Hare, Hare,

Hare Rama, Hare Rama, Rama, Rama, Hare, Hare.

It was Prabhupada's belief that breaking the cycle of samsara—the indefinite cycle of reincarnation—was attained by sankirtana, or the chanting of the names of God, which would bring about "Krishna consciousness." Krishna was held not simply as an incarnation of Vishnu, but as the supreme god. Prabhupada himself said on many occasions that the Hare Krishna movement was not a branch of the Hindu religion but something entirely new and different.

The Future of Hinduism

One important aspect of Hinduism sets it apart from other world religions. As a general rule, Hindus do not proselytize their faith. There are

A Hare Krishna devotee in Michigan leads devotional worship at a shrine in his home.

Hindu teachers outside India; there are ashrams and yoga centers in major cities around the world; but there are no Hindu missionaries. The conversion of outsiders to their particular way of living and faith—their dharma—does not interest Hindu believers.

Nevertheless, many Hindu writers and thinkers see their religion as the one most suited to the future, the faith to which people should turn to resolve certain serious dangers, particularly military and nuclear threats. A speech given by Anandshankar Pandya at the World Hindu Conference sums up this point of view:

Hinduism stands for unity in diversity. Hinduism respects all religions hence generates peace. It also stands for the co-existence and peaceful evolutions of all religious, political, social and economic systems of the world without any coercion because Hinduism is the mother of all religions and cultures and is the only ray of hope in this violent world full of hatred towards each other's religion.

Religious conversion creates tension and hatred among different races. Hence converting others to its religion and destroying their place of worship is a dirty act in the eyes of Hinduism.[67]

What solutions can Hindus offer to the challenges facing their religion and India? A respected religious authority, Sri Jayendra Saraswati, gives another possibility: a conservative change of heart among Indians:

There was a time when the country met all its requirements of food, clothing and shelter, from native enterprises. . . . We need to go back to promoting our rural industries to rid ourselves of all the present ills. . . . If the Government provides the same facilities to native enterprises and the non-resident Indians as they seem to be offering to [Western] multinational

[companies], business opportunities will improve and those wishing to go abroad would stay on. Not only that, even those currently staying abroad would want to come back.[68]

This opinion strikes many Indians as wishful thinking, however. In a nation of more than a billion people, it seems unlikely that such home industries can meet the needs of the entire population. Western influences, in the form of business investment and entertainment, are finding a welcome home on the Indian subcontinent, even while outside religions are not. Most Indians also realize that modern nations cannot do business in isolation. Foreign trade, even as it brings foreign influences, also brings a rising standard of living, an important goal in a nation where the majority of people live in serious poverty.

Shashi Tharoor views the dilemma and the future with optimism:

We can drink Coca-Cola without becoming Coca-colonized. I do not believe that Indians will become any less Indian if, in Mahatma Gandhi's metaphor, we open the doors and windows of our country and let foreign winds blow through our house. Our popular culture has proved resilient enough to compete successfully with MTV and McDonalds; there is probably a greater prospect of our music and movies corrupting foreign youth, especially in other Asian and African countries and among subcontinental expatriate communities in the developed world, than of the reverse.[69]

Hindus still look on their religion as the world's oldest faith, one that links people throughout Asia and Europe to their remote ancestors, the Indo-Europeans. To adapt this religion to the needs of a more interconnected and secular world has become the most serious challenge to Hinduism, but a challenge it seems well suited to meet.

Notes

Introduction: The Elusive Faith

1. Bruce M. Sullivan, *Historical Dictionary of Hinduism*. Lanham, MD: Scarecrow Press, 1997, p. 3.
2. Joseph Campbell, *Baksheesh and Brahman: Indian Journal 1954–55*. New York: HarperCollins, 1995, p. 261.
3. Indira Gandhi, *Eternal India*. New York: Vendome Press, 1980, p. 100.

Chapter 1: The Origins of the Hindu Faith

4. Sinharaja Tammita-Delgoda, *A Traveller's History of India*. New York: Interlink, 1999, pp. 24–25.
5. Quoted in Sanderson Beck, "Vedas and Upanishads," www.san.beck.org/EC7-Vedas.html#2.
6. Burton Stein, *A History of India*. Blackwell History of the World series. Oxford: Blackwell, 1998, pp. 53–54.
7. Tammita-Delgoda, *A Traveller's History of India*, p. 41.
8. Sullivan, *Historical Dictionary of Hinduism*, p. 7.
9. K.M. Sen, *Hinduism*. Baltimore: Penguin Books, 1961, p. 48.
10. Quoted in Stein, *A History of India*, p. 53.
11. D.J. Melling, "Verbal Combat in the Brahmanas," www.nalanda.demon.co.uk/verbal.htm#RitualRiddles.
12. Mark Naidis, *India: A Short Introductory History*. New York: Macmillan, 1966, pp. 12–13.

Chapter 2: The Hindu Gods and Epics

13. Bridget and Raymond Allchin, *The Rise of Civilization in India and Pakistan*. Cambridge, England: Cambridge University Press, 1992, p. 307.
14. Louis Renou, ed., *Hinduism: The Spirit of Hinduism, Its Mythology, Philosophy, Religious and Moral Practices, and Beliefs*. New York: G. Braziller, 1961, p. 141.
15. From the *Mahabharata*, Anusasana Parva, quoted at www.hinduism.co.za/cowsare.htm.
16. Tammita-Delgoda, *A Traveller's History of India*, p. 39.
17. Quoted in V.P. (Hemant) Kanitkar and W. Owen Cole, *Hinduism*. Teach Yourself Books. Lincolnwood, IL: NTC, 1995, p. 106.
18. Sen, *Hinduism*, p. 74.
19. Karel Werner, *A Popular Dictionary of Hinduism*. Lincolnwood, IL: NTC, 1997, p. 45.
20. Stein, *A History of India*, p. 84.
21. Werner, *A Popular Dictionary of Hinduism*, p. 175.
22. Kanitkar and Cole, *Hinduism*, pp. 27–28.
23. Campbell, *Baksheesh and Brahman*, p. 266.
24. Dolf Hartsuiker, *Sadhus: India's Mystic Holy Men*. Rochester, VT: Inner Traditions, 1993, p. 21.

25. J.A. Dubois, *Hindu Manners, Customs and Ceremonies*. Oxford: Clarendon Press, 1959, p. 628.

26. Hartsuiker, *Sadhus*, p. 41.

27. Margaret and James Stutley, *Harper's Dictionary of Hinduism*. New York: Harper & Row, 1977, p. 137.

28. Kanitkar and Cole, *Hinduism*, p. 35.

29. From Chapter 4, Bhagavad Gita, translated at Ishwar.com, www.ishwar.com/shri_bhagwad_gita/chapter04.html.

Chapter 3: The Spread and Development of Hinduism

30. Pandharinath H. Prabhu, *Hindu Social Organization: A Study in Socio-Psychological and Ideological Foundations*. Bombay: Popular Prakashan, 1963, p. 81.

31. Prabhu, *Hindu Social Organization*, p. 83.

32. Quoted in Margaret Cormack and Kiki Skagen, eds., *Voices from India*. New York: Praeger, 1972, p. 57.

33. Tammita-Delgoda, *A Traveller's History of India*, p. 83.

34. Quoted in Renou, *Hinduism*, p. 171.

35. Stein, *A History of India*, p. 145.

36. Kanitkar and Cole, *Hinduism*, p. 149.

37. Campbell, *Baksheesh and Brahman*, p. 261.

Chapter 4: The Practice of Hinduism

38. Quoted in Cormack and Skagen, *Voices from India*, pp. 44–45.

39. Quoted in Sen, *Hinduism*, p. 35.

40. Quoted in Cormack and Skagen, *Voices from India*, p. 45.

41. Sudheer Birodkar, "Diwali, Dassera and Holi," www.hindubooks.org/sudheer_birodkar/hindu_history/festivals1.html.

42. Hema Nair, "A Day of Play," Beliefnet, www.beliefnet.com/story/15/story_1591.html.

43. Satguru Sivaya Subramuniyaswami, "A Hindu Answer to the December Dilemma," Beliefnet, www.beliefnet.com/story/59/story_5965.html.

44. Kanitkar and Cole, *Hinduism*, p. 82.

45. Prabhu, *Hindu Social Organization*, p. 223.

46. Kanitkar and Cole, *Hinduism*, p. 96.

47. Dubois, *Hindu Manners, Customs and Ceremonies*, p. 282.

48. Kanitkar and Cole, *Hinduism*, p. 22.

Chapter 5: Hinduism in the Modern World

49. Arathi Subramanian, "A Discussion with Young American Hindus," www.asia.si.edu/pujaonline/puja/discussion.html.

50. Quoted in Renou, *Hinduism*, p. 234.

51. Stein, *A History of India*, p. 56.

52. Kanitkar and Cole, *Hinduism*, pp. 75–76.

53. Swami Vivekenanda, "The Divine Life Society," www.sivanandadlshq.org/messages/caste.htm.

54. Sullivan, *Historical Dictionary of Hinduism*, pp. 154–55.

55. Quoted in Cormack and Skagen, *Voices from India*, p. 254.

56. Quoted in D. Sampathkumar, "Prosperity Without Faith Is Not Enduring," The Hindu, www.indiaserver.com/businessline/2000/08/11/stories/041144in.htm.

57. Sasthi Brata, *India: Labyrinths in the Lotus Land.* New York: William Morrow, 1985, p. 44.

58. Brata, *India*, p. 45.

59. Raghubir Singh, *The Ganges.* New York: Aperture, 1992, pp. 21–22.

Chapter 6: Modern Challenges to Hinduism

60. Sullivan, *Historical Dictionary of Hinduism*, p. 3.

61. Ankur Shah, "Epic Enemies: A Discussion of Hindu-Muslim Relations in India," http://members.aol.com/megxyz/ankur.html.

62. Shashi Tharoor, *India: From Midnight to the Millennium.* New York: Arcade, 1997, p. 325.

63. Tharoor, *India*, pp. 183–84.

64. Shoba Narayan, "Indian or Hindu: One, Both, or Neither?" www.beliefnet.com/story...?story_8093_1.html.

65. "Why Do Hindus Say, 'I Am Not a Hindu'?" *Hinduism Today,* http://surrealist.org/betrayalofthespirit/iskconhindu.html.

66. Quoted in "Why Do Hindus Say, 'I Am Not a Hindu'?"

67. Anandshankar Pandya, "Hinduism in the Modern World," www.hinduindia.net/frank.html.

68. Quoted in D. Sampathkumar, "Prosperity Without Faith Is Not Enduring," Business Line Internet Edition, www.indiaserver.com/businessline/2000/08/11/stories/041144in.htm.

69. Tharoor, *India*, p. 361.

Glossary

ahimsa: The doctrine of nonviolence and noninjury to living things, followed by many Hindus who carry out their belief through strict vegetarianism.

Aryans: Name given to a migratory group that, according to some historians, originated in the plains of what is now southern Russia and moved into the Indus River Valley some time after 2000 B.C.

ashram: A Hindu religious school.

asramas: Name given to the four stages of life among Hindus: brahmacarya (student); garhasthya (householder); vanaprasthya (retiree); sannyasi (seeker).

atman: The soul, in many Hindu philosophies identical with the Brahman, or all-pervading divine essence of the universe.

avatar: A manifestation of a Hindu divinity in human or animal form.

bhakti: A sect of passionate and devoted followers of particular gods and avatars in Hinduism, and which gradually supplanted the secret religious knowledge and practices of the Vedic priests.

Brahman: Member of the priestly class in ancient India; or of the varna (class) that lies at the head of the caste system still followed by practicing Hindus.

Dalit: Current term for those whose impure occupation places them outside of the Hindu caste system, and who were formerly known as "untouchables."

dharma: The way of right livelihood, action, and worship followed by a practicing Hindu.

jati: A single professional class within the Hindu caste system.

karma: The system of action and consequences within the doctrine of samsara, which holds that karma determines the fate of the soul, or atman, through its series of reincarnations.

moksha: Escape from the cycle of reincarnation, a goal sought by all Hindus.

rishis: Ancient seers held in the highest regard in the Vedic religion of ancient India.

sadhu: A wandering ascetic or holy man.

samsara: In Hindu belief, the cycle of reincarnation and rebirth experienced by the soul.

sanatana-dharma: The way of life, a term used by practicing Hindus to indicate their religion.

sannyasi: A Hindu who has reached the final stage of life, in which worldly duties and ambitions are completely renounced and the individual seeks spiritual enlightenment

Sanskrit: A language used by the high-ranking priestly class in ancient India, and in which many of the Hindu scriptures and epics are written.

shruti: Term applied to the earliest texts of Hinduism, believed to have been "heard" directly from a divine source.

smriti: Term applied to the "remembered" sacred texts of Hinduism, which were set down by humans.

soma: A drink said, in the ancient Vedic religion, to aid the user to achieve enlightenment, visions, and magical abilities.

trimurti: The pantheon of three principal Hindu divinities: Brahman, Vishnu, and Shiva.

upanayana: A ceremony that marks the passage of a young Hindu to the stage of life when he is ready to hear, see, and learn the doctrines of his faith.

varna: One of the four main caste divisions of Hindu society, including brahmins, kshatriyas, vaisyas, and shudras.

Vedic: Name for the sacrificial religion of ancient India that forms the foundation of

Organizations to Contact

American Hindu Foundation
PO Box 2881
Clarksville, IN 47131
An American spiritual group that incorporates the ideals, philosophy, and meditational practices of traditional Hinduism.

Congress of Arya Samajs in North America
24467 Orchard Lake Rd.
Farmington Hills, MI 48336
An organization dedicated to a return to the original teachings of the Vedas and ridding Hinduism of what its leaders perceive to be unhealthy later additions, such as the caste system, and factionalism.

Hindu University of America
PO Box 677906
Orlando, FL 32825
Recently founded in Florida, this institution offers instruction in many different aspects of the Hindu religion, culture, and way of life.

Ramakrishna Vedanta Society
58 Deerfield St.
Boston, MA
An organization that offers lectures, courses, publications, and individual guidance based on the teachings of Sri Ramakrishna and his disciple Swami Vivekenanda, modern Hindu philosophers who have gained a wide following in the West.

World Hindu Council of America
PO Box 441505
Houston, TX 77244
A nonprofit charitable organization serving the needs of all communities originating in India, including Hindus, Jains, Sikhs, Buddhists, as well as practicing Hindus in the United States.

For Further Reading

Alain Danielou, *The Myths and Gods of India: The Classic Work on Hindu Polytheism from the Princeton Bollingen Series*. Rochester, VT: Inner Traditions International, 1992. A description of the Hindu deities and of the myths and philosophies of Hinduism, illustrated with images of the gods.

Ram Dass, *Be Here Now*. New York: Crown, 1971. A Harvard professor and psychiatrist drops out from the West, accepts and adopts the teachings of yoga, describes his discoveries in rambling parables, and exhorts readers to a spiritual awakening and the contemplative life. In general, the counterculture best-seller is an interesting example of the collision of Western culture and Eastern religion.

Krishna Dharma, *Ramayana*. Badger, CA: Torchlight Publishing, 2000. A novelized and abridged translation of the epic story of Rama's journey, written in contemporary English, by an author who has also translated the *Mahabharata*.

Eknath Easwaran, trans., *The Bhagavad Gita*. New York: Vintage, 2000. A selective translation of eighteen chapters of the Bhagavad Gita, one of Hinduism's most powerful and influential works, covering the highlights of the tale of Prince Arjuna and Lord Krishna.

D. Flood, *An Introduction to Hinduism*. Cambridge, England: Cambridge University Press, 1996. A description of the roots and history of Hinduism, emphasizing ritual, influences from the pre-Vedic Dravidian culture, and the tantric philosophy. The author incorporates recent theories and debates on the ancient history of Hinduism and the Aryan migration.

Mohandas Gandhi, *An Autobiography: The Story of My Experiments with Truth*. Boston: Beacon Press, 1993. Gandhi's account of his early activism against colonialism and racism in South Africa and how he came to accept the doctrines of nonviolence and simple living.

John Keay, *India: A History*. New York: Grove, 2001. Going back about five thousand years, this summary of Indian history traces the many conflicts and divisions that made India a ripe prospect for European colonization.

George Michell, *The Hindu Temple: An Introduction to Its Meaning and Forms*. New York: Harper & Row, 1977. A standard work on Hindu religious architecture, giving photographs, plans, and drawings to illustrate the symbolism of the classical temple.

Subramuniya et al., *Dancing with Shiva: Hinduism's Contemporary Catechism*. Kapaa, HI: Himalayan Academy, 1997. A useful and well-organized reference book on Hinduism, with a thorough time line, a glossary of Hindu terms, and a primer on Hinduism for younger readers.

Ed Viswanathan, *Am I a Hindu? The Hinduism Primer.* San Francisco: Halo, 1992. A lively and plain-spoken introduction to Hindu beliefs, simplifying its most esoteric doctrines and answering Westerners' most common questions about Hinduism.

Swami Vivekenanda, *Raja-Yoga.* New York: Ramakrishna Vivekenanda Center, 1980. An introduction to Raja ("royal") Yoga that explains the doctrines of this philosophy in progressively more complex chapters. Explanations of the basic principles of dharma and reincarnation, and a description of Hindu teachings on mental concentration and meditation.

Karel Werner, *A Popular Dictionary of Hinduism.* Lincolnwood, IL: NTC, 1997. A compilation of important Hindu terms, ideas, and names of deities.

Paramahansa Yogananda, *Autobiography of a Yogi.* Los Angeles: Self-Realization Fellowship, 1994. Account of a Hindu teacher who introduced many of the principles of yoga and Hinduism to the West in the first half of the twentieth century.

Heinrich Zimmer and Joseph Campbell, *Myths and Symbols in Indian Art and Civilization.* Princeton, NJ: Princeton University Press, 1972. A hefty and often obscure account of India's most important myths and folklore, and instruction in the symbolism of Indian art and architecture.

Works Consulted

Books

Bridget and Raymond Allchin, *The Rise of Civilization in India and Pakistan.* Cambridge, England: Cambridge University Press, 1982. Scholarly account of the archaeological study of ancient India, and a description of the earliest cities and organized states of the Indus River Valley.

Sasthi Brata, *India: Labyrinths in the Lotus Land.* New York: William Morrow, 1985. A voyage through India conducted by a Westernized Indian journalist, who provides his own family history in the context of modern India's problems and complexities.

Joseph Campbell, *Baksheesh and Brahman: Indian Journal 1954–55.* New York: HarperCollins, 1995. A tour of India and Indian culture with the renowned teacher and scholar of the world's myths and symbols.

Margaret Cormack and Kiki Skagen, eds., *Voices from India.* New York: Praeger, 1972. A collection of narratives written and spoken by Indians of all ages on their lives, their society, and their religion.

J.A. Dubois, *Hindu Manners, Customs and Ceremonies.* Oxford: Clarendon Press, 1959. A French cleric describes Hindu ceremonies and customs firsthand, while traveling through India in the early nineteenth century.

Mircea Eliade, ed., *The Encyclopedia of Religion.* Vol. 6. New York: Macmillan, 1987. Multivolume reference work on major and minor world religions, sects, beliefs, and practices, with a useful essay "Hinduism."

William H. Frederick and Robert L. Worden, *Indonesia: A Country Study.* Washington, DC: Federal Research Division, Library of Congress, 1992. A handbook for diplomats and tourists, covering in great detail modern Indonesia and the country's history and society.

Indira Gandhi, *Eternal India.* New York: Vendome Press, 1980. Illustrated survey of modern India, written by the postcolonial prime minister who led her country through important transformations in the late twentieth century.

Dolf Hartsuiker, *Sadhus: India's Mystic Holy Men.* Rochester, VT: Inner Traditions, 1993. A very interesting and informative photographic essay on the wandering ascetics known as sadhus, who follow a wide variety of doctrines and divide themselves into many different sects.

V.P. (Hemant) Kanitkar and W. Owen Cole, *Hinduism.* Teach Yourself Books. Lincolnwood, IL: NTC, 1995. A description of the basic beliefs, practices, and rituals of modern Hindus, using extensive testimony from Hindu believers and focusing on the Hindu community of Great Britain.

Mark Naidis, *India: A Short Introductory History.* New York: Macmillan, 1966. A brief but comprehensive, clearly written survey of Indian history from the prehistoric Indus Valley civilization to the post-independence years, up to the 1960s.

Pandharinath H. Prabhu, *Hindu Social Organization: A Study in Socio-Psychological and Ideological Foundations.* Bombay: Popular Prakashan, 1963. An in-depth study of Hindu beliefs and systems, such as the ashramas and samskaras, their origins in the distant past, and their meaning for modern Hindus.

Louis Renou, ed., *Hinduism: The Spirit of Hinduism, Its Mythology, Philosophy, Religious and Moral Practices, and Beliefs.* New York: G. Braziller, 1961. A book consisting of an introductory essay on Hinduism and a collection of excerpts from the holy writings, including the Rig-Veda, the Upanishads, the *Mahabharata,* the *Ramayana,* the Puranas, and non-Sanskrit sources. A good introduction to Hindu literature.

K.M. Sen, *Hinduism.* Baltimore: Penguin Books, 1961. A brief account of Hinduism, focusing on the development of different Hindu beliefs and schools of thought through Indian history.

Raghubir Singh, *The Ganges.* New York: Aperture, 1992.

Burton Stein, *A History of India.* Blackwell History of the World series. Oxford: Blackwell, 1998. Lengthy, scholarly, and very detailed description of Indian history, covering all aspects of Indian geography, literature, culture, and religion.

Margaret and James Stutley, *Harper's Dictionary of Hinduism.* New York: Harper & Row, 1977. Comprehensive, scholarly reference book of Hindu terms and the mythologies associated with the various Hindu gods.

Bruce M. Sullivan, *Historical Dictionary of Hinduism.* Lanham, MD: Scarecrow Press, 1997. Clear and concise definitions of hundreds of terms and concepts associated with Hinduism, along with a useful introduction to the subject.

Sinharaja Tammita-Delgoda, *A Traveller's History of India.* New York: Interlink, 1999. Concise and very useful overview of Indian history, from the ancient past to independence in the twentieth century. Covers important art styles, philosophical ideas, architecture, literature, and religion.

Shashi Tharoor, *India: From Midnight to Millennium.* New York: Arcade, 1997. An Indian novelist and playwright addresses culture, politics, and religion in modern India. Tharoor vividly describes foreign influences in India and asserts that India holds the solution to problems and challenges faced by the rest of the world in the next century.

Internet Sites

The Arthur M. Sackler and Freer Gallery of Art (**www.asia.si.edu**). A site dedicated to events, lectures, performances, and exhibitions at the Smithsonian Institution's gallery of Asian art.

Beliefnet (**www.beliefnet.com**). A useful, encyclopedic, and well-organized source on the world's major religions, describing their prinicpal tenets and beliefs, modern practice, issues and problems, opinion articles, and links.

The Darshana Indian Philosophy Page (**www.nalanda.demon.co.uk**). A series of informative essays on the various schools and philosophies of Hinduism, some current and some purely historical, as well as a few links to other important Hinduism sites.

The Divine Life Society (**www.sivanan dadlshq.org**). Dedicated to the teachings of the founder of the Divine Life Society, Sri Swami Sivanandaji Maharaj.

"Epic Enemies: A Discussion of Hindu-Muslim Relations in India" (**http://members.aol.com/megxyz/ankur.html.**) An essay by AOL member Ankur Shah on the age-old religious conflict within India.

Hindubooks (**www.hindubooks.org**). A collection of full-length works on Hindu religion and Indian history.

HinduIndia (**www.hinduindia.net**). As stated on the home page, "The aim of this web site is to create permanent peace, happiness, material prosperity & socio-economic harmony of the human race by propagating the eternal, spiritual and natural truth of Dharma which sustain human society. That truth is HINDUISM."

India in New York (**www.indiain newyork.com**). A site dedicated to news, reviews, happenings and interests among the Indian-American population of New York City.

Ishwar.com (**www.ishwar.com**). Maintained by software entrepreneur Ishwar Joshi, this website contains religious texts for seven major religions: Buddhism, Christianity, Islam, Judaism, Jainism, Hinduism, and Sikhism.

Itihaas (**www.itihaas.com**). Articles, links, time lines, and much more on Indian history, religion, and culture, along with useful links to modern India-related services, including "Live Cricket on the Net."

The Literary Works of Sanderson Beck (**www.san.beck.org**). A collection of essays in philosophy, spirituality, Eastern and Western religions, ethics, and current events by a teacher at the World University in Ojai, California, and reviver of the University of the Golden Age, a free university founded in 1973 and now located on the Internet.

Resource for Religious Texts (**www.ishwar. com**). Complete translations of the key books of the major world faiths, including Hinduism's Bhagavad Gita.

Understanding Hinduism (**www.hin duism.co.za**). A site containing a large number of highly informative articles on topics relating to Hinduism.

Index

Picture Credits

© Steve Allen/Brand X Pictures/PictureQuest, 67
AP/Wide World, 26, 38, 43, 49, 61, 63, 72, 73, 82, 84, 91, 77
AP/Wide World/The Manassas Journal Messenger, 55
© Christie's Images/CORBIS, 31
Corbisimages, 34
© M. Freeman/PhotoLink/PhotoDisc, 37
© Arvind Garg/CORBIS, 36
© Lindsay Hebberd/CORBIS, 54
© Historical Picture Archive/CORBIS, 21
© Robert Holmes/CORBIS, 17
Hulton/Archive by Getty Images, 58, 69, 79
© Travel Ink/CORBIS, 10
© Earl and Nazima Kowall/CORBIS, 9, 74
Boudot-Lamotte, 14 (right)
© Charles and Josette Lenars/CORBIS, 19, 57
© Michael S. Lewis/CORBIS, 41
Brandy Noon, 13
© Roger Ressmeyer/CORBIS, 50
© C. Sherburne/PhotoLink/PhotoDisc, 45
© David H. Wells/CORBIS, 65
© Roger Wood/CORBIS, 14 (left)

About the Author

Thomas Streissguth has written more than 30 books of non-fiction for young readers, from Life Among the Vikings to Utopian Visionaries; Lewis and Clark; Wounded Knee: The end of the Plains Indian Wars; and the award-winning Hustlers and Hoaxers. He has written or collaborated on dozens of geography books as well as biographies and descriptive histories. His interests include music, languages, and travel. He has also co-founded a private language school, "Learn French!", which hosts summer tours each year in Europe. He lives in Florida with his wife and two daughters.